MULTIPLIERS
Leading Beyond Addition

by Todd Wilson

Foreword by Carl George

an Exponential Series Resource

Special Thanks

Lindy Lowry for her amazing writing and editing skills. This book would not have happened without her long hours and keen knowledge of Exponential's multiplication content.

The growing number of Multipliers I have the privilege of calling friends, who share a heartfelt passion and camaraderie for seeing the percentage of U.S. churches that ever reproduce increase from less than 4 percent to greater than 10 percent.

The Exponential 2017/2018 Multipliers Group (approximately 150 leaders) who are using this book as a guide for pursuing Level 5 multiplication.

Bob and Linda Buford for investing in the next generation of Level 5 Multipliers and for helping pour gas on this vital conversation.

Dave Ferguson and Warren Bird for their work in creating the new book *Hero Maker: 5 Essential Practices for Leaders to Multiply Leaders* (Zondervan – early 2018), the theme Exponential 2018 and the context for this new *Multipliers* book. Dave was instrumental in the development of Chapter 7 on Hero Making.

The entire Exponential Team for sacrificially serving church multiplication leaders and stepping up to do whatever was needed, whenever it was needed, to finish this resource and to serve church Multipliers.

HeroMaker Events

This book is one of several Exponential Series Resources that highlights the vital importance of changing the scorecard of leaders in the church in the US. To see multiplication movements, we must first see leaders who die to themselves and embrace scorecards of "hero-making." We must move from being heroes of our own stories to becoming hero-makers in God's story.

The 2018 Exponential Theme is HeroMaker. Join us at one of our six HeroMaker events, starting with our national event in Orlando, Florida. Additional regional events provide opportunities to bring your entire team to an event closer to home.

www.exponential.org/events

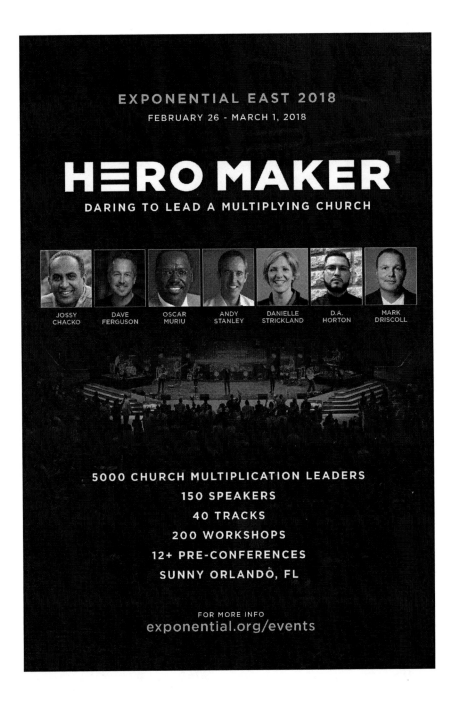

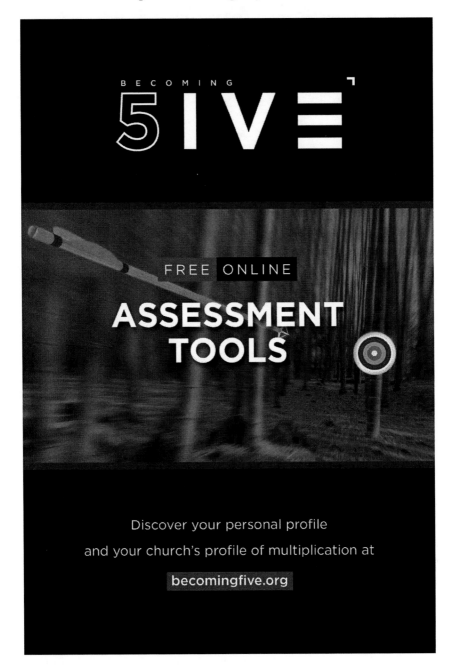

exponential.org

Special Invitation

This book is a taste of our 2018 HeroMaker theme. Please consider attending one of our six Exponential 2018 events. Our goal is to help shape your paradigm for multiplication, inspire and encourage you to multiply, and equip you to turn ideas into action. Our 2018 conferences are built on the content of this book, and are designed to help you move from ideas and inspiration to implementation and impact.

2018 Theme: HeroMaker: Daring to Lead a Multiplying Church

Locations and dates: Our national conference, Exponential in Orlando, Florida, is a full-service event with thousands of attendees, 150+ speakers, 40 tracks, 200 workshops, and 12+ pre-conference equipping labs. Our Exponential regional events are shorter and geographically based (translating to lower overall costs for large teams). Regionals bring the full "punch" of the national conferences' five main stage sessions without the breakout workshops.

2018 National HeroMaker Event
Exponential // Orlando, Florida // February 26 – March 1, 2018

2018 Regional HeroMaker Events
Washington DC, Southern CA, Northern CA, Chicago IL, and Houston TX

exponential.org

Inside

Foreword
By Carl George

I've been leading ministry and working with church planters for more than thirty years now, and I could not be more excited about what I'm seeing going on with Exponential. This is the finest program for church planters that I've ever seen. I organized my first church planter conference with Peter Wagner at Fuller in 1983, but only this year (2017) did I get to attend my first Exponential event. I was newly energized by what I saw there as I realized what Exponential represents to the Church. Dave Ferguson and Todd Wilson are encouraging and exhorting young pastors to find ways of galvanizing action toward new church plants from the very beginning of their ministry during those initial formation stages *before* they hit various attendance plateaus.

With this important focus on multiplication, Exponential is attempting to accomplish what we were hoping to do at the birth of the Church Growth movement. We really wanted to see multiplication happen, but we were missing a key ingredient that is the essence of Exponential. Going forward, my dream is to see the fulfillment of their vision and move beyond the prevailing addition scorecard in the U.S, Church to a scorecard focused on multiplication.

In my younger years, my wife and I started several church plants by accident. In retrospect, I wish I had understood then that we could have built multiplication into our ministry DNA. What I'm now seeing is that church planters can actually be intentional (and *should* be intentional) about planting and sponsoring new churches even as they are starting. After studying what Exponential is doing, I realized that the notion that a new church planter could simultaneously be a new church plant sponsor had never entered my mind. Our ministry led to both planting and sponsoring, but the sponsored churches were results of solving other disciple making issues. We were focused on obedience to make disciples, but the planting of more churches was almost incidental to that. It did not occur to us to focus on it.

If I could go back and start over again, I would want to imitate Ralph Moore and be intentional from the very beginning about having a scorecard for multiplication. So I encourage you, church leader, to take advantage of what it took me thirty years to wake up to. With Exponential's Level 5 concept, you get the benefit of creating a scorecard of multiplication and starting out with a multiplication orientation from the earliest days of your ministry.

This book you are holding is a fantastic roadmap for you as you begin or move forward on this multiplication journey—if you'll take it to head and heart. It's the manual I wish I had when we were starting out. I'm excited that Exponential has taken several years of multiplication content and has cohesively pulled it into this single handbook that every church leader aspiring to become a Multiplier can use to guide them as they create a scorecard and vision for multiplication, and ultimately a culture of multiplying churches.

Church planting leaves quite a legacy. The idea that a newly planted church can have among its intended purposes the starting of additional churches is a tremendously important mind and heart shift, as you'll learn through this book. When a pastor and a group of church leaders determine that they're going to deliberately and intentionally plant and sponsor church plants, more new churches result, and the Church advances.

I look forward to seeing and learning about you and the churches you multiply as you pursue what God has called and gifted you to do!

Carl George
Author, Analyst, and Coach

Introduction

As Exponential kicks off our 2018 theme, "HeroMaker," we're turning our attention to the individual *leader*. With no multiplication movements in the United States, we obviously have a leadership problem and a scorecard problem. We desperately need Level 5 leaders to emerge who can catalyze movements of Level 5 multiplying churches. If we're going to make a difference and move the multiplication needle from less than 4 percent of churches ever reproducing to greater than 10 percent, we need to start with a new scorecard and paradigm for success, and that change must start in the heart and practices of the individual leader.

Exponential is championing the call for Level 5 **Multipliers** to rise up in the emerging generation, and to lead us down a new path. A future where multiplication is the fruit of a renewed focus on biblical disciple making and an intentionality to deploy rather than accumulate. This outcome will require leaders to shift their primary role from being the hero of their local church to becoming the hero maker of others who are released and sent to repeat the cycle.

I know it's hard to imagine, but the largest and most influential churches in America, led by remarkable leaders like Rick Warren, Bill Hybels, Craig Groeschel, and Andy Stanley, will eventually experience the same fate as your church—subtraction leading to death. For over 2,000 years, the lifespan of greater than 99.9 percent of all local churches is less than 100 years (most are less than 50 years)!

Don't believe me? Can you name just one local church still around today that existed in the first century? I can't! So, given the truth that local churches have a finite lifespan, and that you have a limited number of years to make the biggest impact possible, why would you choose the pursuit of accumulation as your strategy?

The greatest movement in the history of the world has been carried through the centuries by millions of local churches, each with a birth and then an inevitable death. With the same Kingdom math that applies to your church, the legacy of all 300,000-plus churches in the United States will ultimately be measured not by what they accumulated during their 100-year (or less) lifespan, but rather by what they released and sent. It's the sending behaviors, not the accumulating pursuits, which have brought your church into existence and are the critical element of Jesus' plan for carrying His fullness to the ends of the earth.

The uncomfortable truth is that our prevailing scorecards for success are wrong. Right now, 96 percent of the estimated 300,000-plus Christian churches in the United States have never planted a single church. If we applied that same math to human reproduction, the results would be disastrous.

These numbers beg the critical question: *Why?* Why is almost every U.S. church ignoring or neglecting the multiplication plan that Jesus set in motion for His Church when He gave His Great Commission (Matt. 28:18-20) and called us to make disciples who would be His witnesses "to the ends of the earth" (Acts 1:8)?

The next generation needs Multipliers—leaders who will challenge the status quo and seek to throw off the shackles of accumulation-based scorecards and prevailing paradigms that are so ideally suited for producing cultural Christians. This book is about putting to death our unhealthy thinking and paradigms. It's about embracing a new scorecard and creating a vision for, and culture of, multiplication. It's about calling leaders to become the Multipliers that God has called us to be.

I can't tell you how thrilled I am that you're on this journey to becoming a Level 5 Multipliers! Since Exponential's launch in 2006, we have come alongside church leaders to inspire, challenge and equip them to multiply disciple makers. We are a community of activists who believes that church multiplication is the best way to carry out Jesus' Great Commission and expand God's Kingdom. We dream of movements of Level 5 Multipliers mobilized with new scorecards, new values, and new mindsets into every corner of society.

This new book is an anchor resource supporting our 2018 HeroMaker theme. It pulls the core and best content from our previous resources into a single new resource, while adding important new content for leaders who are pursuing Level 5 leadership. We've pulled from and aggregated the best of the learnings from our three multiplication-focused anchor books: *Spark: Igniting a Culture of Multiplication, Becoming a Level 5 Multiplying Church,* and *Dream Big, Plan Smart: Finding Your Pathway to Level 5 Multiplication.*

Leading beyond addition toward multiplication requires every leader to experience an "aha" awakening that while your church may be growing, you need a new scorecard that values multiplication and Kingdom growth above more limiting accumulation-based cultures. Ultimately, our prayer and passion are to see individual leaders commit to deconstructing their current paradigms of success and use a new scorecard.

Because change must start in the heart of *you.*

You are perfectly positioned, amid all your struggles and tensions, to be a Multiplier—to move from being a hero focused on building a Level 3 addition-based church, to becoming a hero maker who pursues Level 5 multiplication by investing in and releasing others.

Will you become a Multiplier who leads beyond addition?

exponential.org

Chapter 1
Reality Check

Is what you're living for worth Jesus dying for?
~ Oscar Muriu

I'm assuming that you're reading this book because you're passionate about seeing God's Kingdom grow and advance, and are committed to becoming a Level 5 Multiplier. Making such a life- and church-changing shift isn't easy. It requires us to face some sobering realities and confront how we define success, and then discern how that definition is driving our current scorecard.

Allow this chapter to be a self-assessment of sorts to help you reflect on your church's foundation. Is it a foundation aligned to produce disciples and multiplication? Or are you set up to produce converts and cultural Christians? What adjustments are needed?

The Search for 'Radically Multiplying' Churches

It's easy to find wildly successful churches doing all the right things for addition growth. It's far more difficult to find radically multiplying churches like Ralph Moore's Hope Chapel that are experiencing and igniting multiplication growth. Today, more than 2,300 churches can trace their roots to the seven churches Ralph started in the 1970s. That's radical multiplication! Far more significant than the current numbers is the reality that these 2,300 churches have multiplication so deeply embedded in their DNA that the resulting additional churches—which will be started over the next 10 years—will likely be mind-blowing.

Let's define "radically multiplying" in a way that's so different and so aggressive—compared with our current paradigms and measures of success—that few people would argue if it were addition or multiplication. The fruit of these churches is such a testimony that these congregations are radically multiplying without the need for a definition.

Several years ago, our Exponential team set out to identify ten radically multiplying U.S. churches—just ten that we could highlight and learn from. With more than 350,000 churches in the United States, that ten represents just .003 percent of churches. We spent months looking and inquiring, but we couldn't find ten. We couldn't find even three.

Something is just not right. If the Church is made to multiply, why don't we see it happening?

With most every problem comes the promise of opportunity and change. As a leader, you're perfectly positioned, amid all your struggles and tensions, to be a change maker and a Multiplier. That may sound counter-intuitive, but it's true. That change starts with embracing new ways of thinking. Moving the needle from less than 4 percent of U.S. churches ever reproducing to greater than 10 percent will take a groundswell of next-generation leaders like you who will look beyond the prevailing measures of addition growth and adopt new scorecards of multiplication growth.

You are creating and cultivating a culture in your church. There is no stopping it. Just as the sun rises and sets each day, your core values and convictions are always there, transforming your thinking into actions that functionally form your church's unique culture. How you face and maneuver through the tensions you experience might be the most significant blessings you have in shaping your church's culture and DNA.

Like the small rudder on a large ship directing the ship's course, the stewardship of the culture/DNA in your church may be the most profound role you play as its leader. Unfortunately, changing an existing culture is not as easy as simply adjusting a rudder. The process of building a healthy culture of multiplication starts with courageous leaders getting honest about their current scorecard.

Our Current State of Affairs

In our 2016 anchor book, *Becoming a Level 5 Multiplying Church*, Exponential laid out five different levels of multiplication to help church leaders determine where they are and where they want to go. Ultimately, these multiplication levels help answer the questions, "Where are we now, and how can we know if we're on the right track?"

As Ed Stetzer says in his foreword to the book, "When leaders grasp the next step to take, it enables movements of multiplication to not only become a goal but an attainable goal and, at some point, a *realized* goal."

Below, we identify the five levels or cultures of multiplication. Read the descriptions and then go to becomingfive.org to take Exponential's FREE online assessment. It will help you identify your church's current level of multiplication and to discern the culture you're aspiring to create in the future.

Level 1: Subtracting

Approximately 80 percent of U.S. churches are subtracting (attendance is decreasing) or have plateaued. This 80 percent stat tells us that the vast majority of churches in the United States exist in a survival culture characterized by scarcity thinking. These churches are living in a culture that simply makes it difficult for them to even *think* about multiplication.

Typically, Level 1 leaders live with financial tensions that produce a scarcity mindset, which shapes their culture and how they approach ministry. These churches struggle to pay a full-time pastor and then strive toward being able to afford their own facility. For leaders of Level 1 churches, planning doesn't look too much beyond getting done what needs to be done for the next couple of weeks. The senior pastor is running hard to keep up with everything, and the exhaustive to-do list doesn't leave much time for developing leaders. The church depends on the weekend gatherings for financial viability. So it's not surprising that the weekend services become the focal point. While there may be talk of growth, most of the energy is spent on keeping up with the needs of people and running Sunday services. Most strategic and vision conversations about the future end with, "We will [fill in the blank] someday when we can afford it." Unfortunately, that elusive day rarely comes for most Level 1 churches and leaders.

Level 2: Plateaued Level 2 leaders are in churches that have survived and may be growing. But these leaders' mindset lies in a state of tension between scarcity and growth. They have growth in their sights with Level 3 at the pinnacle, but their scarcity thinking constrains growth and multiplication. Their focus and aspirations center on growth and addition, and their primary characterizations are, "tension, scarcity, survival, and growth." Level 2 churches are often torn by the tyranny of the *or*: "Now that we're financially stable and holding our own, do we put money into staff *or* a permanent facility?" Lacking vision and values for multiplication, the priority of actually releasing resources to multiply just doesn't measure up to the perceived reward at the top of Level 3.

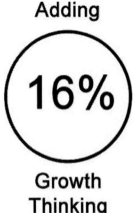

Adding

16%

Growth Thinking

Level 3: Adding *Some 15 to 20 percent of churches that find themselves at Level 3 are growing by addition, not multiplication.*

A Level 3 leader prioritizes growth and is seeing attendance increase. Many Level 3 churches are often externally focused, making an impact in their communities, and many have added multisite venues. Most of the largest and fastest-growing churches that make our "envy lists" are actually Level 3,

22

and their leaders are conquerors with a demonstrated record of taking the next hill. They've grown accustomed to finding and solving problems that limit growth. While these leaders don't *want* to fundamentally be about the numbers, they also know that numbers matter. Income is directly proportional to attendance, and the number of volunteers needed increases as attendance increases.

Level 4: Reproducing *Approximately 4 percent of U.S. churches reproduce programmatically as part of their growth.*

Level 4 leaders sense that there is something more than attendance growth and are drawn to a future that's more about planting new orchards than putting more trees in their orchard. However, while they may aspire to move to Level 5 and might be making progress, too often the tensions and forces pulling them back to Level 3 limit their ability to move more fully to Level 5. Level 4 churches are as passionate about leadership development systems that intentionally produce leaders who "go," as they are about producing systems that develop leaders to stay. They are birthing and taking ownership of a strong value of multiplication, including putting behaviors and practices in place that are consistent with Level 5 churches.

Multiplication

< .1%

Movements

Thinking

Level 5: Multiplying *Currently represented by less than .005 percent of U.S. churches.*

The numbers don't lie. Very few U.S. churches experience a multiplication culture. Level 5 Multipliers pursue planting churches as a normal and regular part of their existence. They continually develop and send people to plant. These leaders plant hundreds of churches and send thousands of people to be part of church-planting teams over their lifespan. Their scorecard is more about "who and how many have been sent" than "how many have been accumulated." Level 5 leaders see their church through a Kingdom lens. Their burden is more for Kingdom capacity than for local church capacity. These rare churches develop a DNA so strongly centered on multiplication that they would have to *try* not to multiply.

Churches with a multiplication culture have broken free from the bondage of Level 3 addition thinking and have put practices in place that close the gap between multiplication behaviors and aspirations. They are courageous leaders who are more burdened by building Kingdom capacity than local church capacity. They are Level 5 Multipliers.

To read full lists of characteristics for each multiplication level, see Appendix A in our free eBook Becoming a Level 5 Multiplying Church, available via exponential.org.

Addicted to Addition

In their book, *Viral Churches: Helping Church Planters Become Movement Makers* (based on findings from Leadership Network's State of Church Planting study), authors Warren Bird and Ed Stetzer give us a vital reality check: "In spite of increased interest in church-planting ventures, there has yet to be a documented church-planting movement, which involves the rapid multiplication of churches rather than the simple addition of churches."[1]

Stetzer and Bird go so far as to call this pursuit of growth an "addiction."

"Our 'viral church' idea is about falling in love with multiplication," they write, "and abandoning what seems to be an addiction to addition."[2]

As a leader, are you addicted to addition growth? Think hard before you answer. What does your current scorecard reveal about your motives? This question might be the single most important one you ask. Our motives tend to define our priorities, behaviors and ultimately, our results. At the highest level, are you driven by addition, reproduction, or multiplication? Are you satisfied being the very best Level 3 church you can be, growing as big as you can and reaching as many people as possible? Or are you seeking to move to Levels 4 and 5 that require a new scorecard? (We'll talk more about motives and your personal scorecard in chapters 6 and 7).

The bottom line is that we're facing an epidemic of addition lust. We've defined the measure of success in the U.S. Church based on the Level 3 scorecard versus Level 5. As missiologist Alan Hirsch writes in *Becoming a Level 5 Multiplying Church*:

"Our definition of success seldom reaches beyond addition-growth. This is important because we generally get what we're aiming for. If all our exemplary churches and leaders are at Level 3, then our standards of success are in fact limiting our missional potential. We need to think much bigger and reach much higher."[3]

As we look toward 2018 and what it means to be a hero maker (a Level 5 Multiplier), we come face-to-face with the truth that our addition-focused scorecards are holding us back from becoming leaders who multiply disciples that birth new communities of faith. Our current scorecard stands in the way of us becoming Level 5 Multipliers.

Regardless of the level you find yourself at today, the important thing is to consider where you are, where you'd like to go, and what you need to change today to move yourself in the right direction. Part of that change will require you to honestly test the foundation of your church. Is Jesus truly the foundation? Or have you built your church on other things? In the coming chapters, we'll look at why our foundation is so key to creating a scorecard that sets us up to become Level 5 Multipliers.

Putting It Into Practice

• *Why are you and your team responding to and engaging in the multiplication conversation now?*

• *How do you measure growth in your church? How do you measure health?*

• *If you wrote your church history as a story, what would the major chapters be about? Who would the heroes be?*

• *In what specific ways do the time and financial resources necessary for overcoming growth barriers in your church compete with multiplication activities? In what ways could they be complementary?*

• *Why is a reality check vitally important for replacing unhealthy addition-focused activities with multiplication activities and values?*

Chapter 2
Leverage

*Give me a lever long enough and a fulcrum on which to place it,
and I shall move the world.*
~Archimedes

Imagine putting one quarter into a vending machine and getting ten out in exchange. Sound too good to be true? Leverage works that way. It multiplies an input to a far greater output. The law of leverage is at work everywhere around us.

For example, the three small hinges on a heavy door let you easily and freely swing the door back and forth with the slightest of effort. Or think about your finances. Invest $50 per month starting at age 18, and you'll likely be a millionaire by retirement. Or, how about the seesaw on a kid's playground? When leverage is applied, a 100-pound child is easily lifted high in the air. Leverage multiplies our labors into far greater fruit than what we could possibly achieve on our own.

Leverage's Multiplying Effect

The ultimate leverage, however, happens when followers of Jesus fully surrender to His Lordship. Consider the impact of twelve ordinary men who took seriously Jesus' command to "go and make disciples." They helped launch the greatest, most sustained movement in the history of the world. This type of leverage multiplies a few loaves and fishes into enough food to feed 5,000 people and an empty fishing net into an overflowing catch.

Looking at this law of leverage, I begin to understand Jesus' promise that I can personally be like good soil that allows God's Word to grow, produce fruit, and multiply thirty, sixty, and even one hundred times in and through my life! Leverage is also why I'm naturally drawn to church multiplication and its potential for impact.

Who wouldn't want to tap into the multiplying effect of leverage? That's why we read the parable of the talents and immediately want to be the five-talent faithful steward who doubles his master's resources into ten talents. It's the stewardship of the faithful manager that prompts the master's commendation. In giving each of us unique gifts (our time, talent and treasure), the Master expects stewardship and faithfulness. Why would we strive for anything less than leveraging these resources thirty, sixty, or even one hundred times what has been entrusted to our care?

And yet, we often settle for so much less.

As we saw in chapter 1, the prevailing scorecard for success in the U.S. Church is rooted in approaches that don't produce multiplication. In fact, these Level 3 addition-focused approaches or strategies can stifle the very leverage that Jesus sought to embed into the DNA of His Church.

Archimedes, the famous mathematician and inventor from ancient Greece, said and proved that leverage requires a properly positioned lever and a fulcrum. In physics terms, a fulcrum is an anchor or foundation through which a lever can transform an input effort into a multiplied output. The simple sketch below how a small effort or force applied on one end of a lever can lift a heavy weight on the other end.

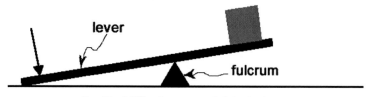

small effort lifts large weight via lever

For leverage to occur, you must have the right lever and it must be positioned on the right fulcrum or foundation. In other words, wrong fulcrum, no multiplication. Wrong lever, no multiplication.

With no real multiplication movements in the United States, I can only conclude we must be embracing the wrong fulcrum and the wrong lever! The following table shows an example of how we might functionally choose the wrong fulcrum and lever in our zeal to pursue Level 3 addition.

	Level 3 Addition	Level 5 Multiplication
Fulcrum	Growth Strategies	Jesus
Lever	Attendance	Disciple Makers

To experience leverage, we need to rediscover and embrace the right elements. Jesus must be our fulcrum, with our lever being faithful, obedient followers who obey His command to, "Go and make disciples." To do that, however, we need to throw off the old wineskins we so desperately hold onto.

Satan does everything within his power to keep us focused on the wrong scorecards and distracted from experiencing the multiplication leverage Jesus intends for us. That's why we're not seeing any measurable movements in the United States. Like the serpent deceiving Adam and Eve, Satan tricks us into believing that success lies just past the next addition growth barrier. We conquer the next hill simply to find another one waiting. He convinces us that accumulation growth is our prize, holding us captive from ever experiencing the leverage that produces multiplication.

Embracing the Call

What our nation needs now, more than ever, are courageous Multipliers who will seek to rediscover and embrace the leverage Jesus intends for us to have—leading beyond addition thinking.

Multipliers take their cues from Jesus and seek to be fruitful and multiply. They are intentional about Jesus' "go and make disciples" command (Matt. 28: 18-20) and fully embrace and embody the leverage that comes from building capacity for disciple making through the multiplication of healthy, reproducing churches. Multipliers embrace a multiplication scorecard that prioritizes releasing and sending over accumulating and growing.

Are you feeling any discontent about our prevailing accumulation cultures? Do you hear the whisper of the Holy Spirit convicting you that something's just not right about our addiction, and possibly idolatry, for accumulation cultures that produces cultural Christians? I'm guessing many of you are.

It's time to embrace the call to become a Multiplier!

Leverage your calling in ways that empower and unleash a movement of biblical disciple makers. This is so critical. When we don't leverage our passion for Jesus' cause, we can become idolaters. Sound harsh? Keep reading.

Putting It into Practice

• *Why is God calling leaders to become Multipliers?*
• *In what ways have you been convinced that success lies past the next addition growth barrier and that accumulation growth is the prize?*
• *When and how did you realize Satan had tricked you?*
• *How did that belief inhibit multiplication?*
• *Are you ready to do the work necessary for becoming a Multiplier? How are you praying to prepare yourself, your team, and your church for the journey ahead?*

Chapter 3
Activism

Activist – one who vigorously advocates for a cause or issue.

I'm an activist. I'm guessing you are, too. In fact, most of our friends, neighbors, peers, and co-workers are activists for something. We live in a time when everyone seems to passionately champion a cause. However, if we're not careful, our activism can simply become a form of idolatry. As we embark on the journey to become Multipliers, we must insist that our activism is properly rooted and placed.

I find myself asking if it's possible that the rise in our activist culture is also a contributing cause of the historic levels of division in our nation? If you're like me, your gut tells you we've gone off track. Too often, our activism is rooted in the wrong motives, using language and strategies inconsistent with the One in whose name we come. As Christians, it's vital that we have a solid biblical foundation for our activism. Otherwise, our activism becomes idolatry. Multipliers are activists, so we must be sure to champion the right cause with the right motives.

I love the phrase that Level 5 Multiplier Ralph Moore uses to describe activists in chapter 1 of his Exponential book (with Jeff Christopherson), *New to Five: Starting a Level 5 Multiplying Church*. Ralph calls himself a "monomaniac with a mission."[1] Monomaniacs are laser-focused with a relentless drive to pursue and accomplish their deeply held burden or conviction. Being a monomaniac with a mission can be profoundly good or profoundly bad. For example, the apostle Paul was a monomaniac, but so was Hitler.

While most of us activists are sincere in our passions and burdens, today's plethora of causes and voices creates a whole lot of unproductive noise. We're fragmented; our individual causes are like planes without an airport. The current context of our activism often seems disconnected from the One we seek to honor.

What if our activism, while rooted in good intentions, is fueled more by our own narcissism than by our faith in God? Is our passion more about our own message than Jesus' gospel? Are we focused more on our voice being heard than proclaiming His Word? Are we more about our scorecard and success than accomplishing Jesus' mission? These are tough questions, but important ones to ask as you start the journey toward becoming a Level 5 Multiplier.

Jesus, an Activist for _____

Recently, I've been studying and reflecting on the activism of Jesus. I challenge you to read all the red-letter words in the four Gospels through the lens of Jesus as an activist. You'll get a fresh perspective. Be careful not to single out individual verses that support your particular cause; look for the underlying thread that runs through His ministry.

What do you find? If you were writing His epitaph—"Jesus, an activist for [fill in the blank]"—what word would you fill in? You only get to pick one or two words. What would they be?

Let's start with the words that would *not* be on the list. Let me make it personal. I'm an activist for church planting and multiplication. I'm willing to give the rest of my life to seeing the percentage of U.S. churches that ever reproduce increase from less than 4 percent to greater than 10 percent. So, it makes sense that I'd like for Jesus' epitaph to end with "church planting and multiplication." In fact, I often act as if it does. My passion would seem to indicate it. So would my impatience with accumulation-focused leaders and churches. But no matter how passionate I am about my cause, Jesus was not primarily an activist for church planting and multiplication. He cares about it, but He knows that if we faithfully and obediently focus on making healthy biblical disciples, we'll get church planting and multiplication as one byproduct of that fruit.

It's sobering to realize that if I elevate my cause to be above His—even if my cause is multiplying His Church—I'm practicing a form of idolatry.

So what about social justice? Racial reconciliation? Urban revitalization and community development? Leadership development? Multiethnic churches? Refugees and immigrants? Environmentalism? LGBTQ rights? Equality? Political ideology? Missional? Church growth?

Nope. They aren't Jesus' core cause either, though He cares deeply about these and other issues. Again, focusing on healthy disciple making as His primary goal and cause will bring much more vibrant results in the other areas we seek to champion.

Tied to a Bigger Cause

At last year's national Multiethnic Church Conference, I had the privilege of spending time with Dr. John Perkins, a former Civil Rights activist and now a stalwart voice in the Church. Our meeting came at a time when I was working on Exponential's 2017 anchor book, *Dream Big, Plan Smart: Finding Your Pathway to Level 5 Multiplication,* and was feeling deeply convicted to learn about the activism of Jesus. I went to the gathering with a listening posture to discern some direction from God.

Dr. Perkins asked me what I thought about the event. I told him that I absolutely loved the passion of the people attending. It was electrifying! These passionate activists could change the world in any area they set their hearts and minds to (I'd actually like to see this kind of passion in the church-planting and multiplication space). I noted that there were five different tribes represented: urban, racial reconciliation, community development, social justice, and multiethnic churches.

Dr. Perkins asked me for critical feedback on the overall progress being made. I didn't want to answer. He insisted.

33

"There's a disconnect for me," I told him. "It feels like five fingers separated from the hand, each finger speaking its own language and doing its own thing. But none of the fingers are tied to a bigger common cause."

I suggested that until the hub of the hand focuses on biblical disciple making, we were likely to spin in circles. At 86 years old, this venerable leader stumbled backward with excitement. He looked at me and said, "That's exactly right. We must make disciple making the main thing that ties everything else together. I plan on giving the rest of my days to that."

Without healthy, biblical disciple making that leads to true heart transformation and deeper surrender to Jesus as Lord, all of our activist causes will be rooted in worldly goodness and pursuits. We will practice a form of idolatry. Jesus gave us a clear, compelling, and *primary* cause—intended to tie together all of our worldly efforts for good.

Jesus, an activist for disciple making! The kind built around the full surrender to His Lordship. The kind that looks different than the world, and in its full maturity has no choice but to multiply and result in people mobilized to make a difference in the world's injustices. We must, however, recognize the truth that our prevailing discipleship systems in place today just aren't leading to multiplication the way He intended. Our causes end up consuming the first fruits of our time, talent and treasure, with disciple making taking on a lower priority.

Jesus came to proclaim that the Kingdom of Heaven is near. In doing so, He gave us a vision and picture of a preferable future. He reminded us of our sinful nature and the chasm between God and us. He proclaimed the Good News of a pathway of hope that moves us from sinners deserving of death to disciples who experience the fullness of eternity. He proclaimed His intention that we not only have life, but that we experience it to the fullest measure (John 10:10).

All of these things were His message. But let me suggest that His method of activism relied on modeling healthy biblical disciple making and commissioning His people to make it *their* main thing! Disciple making ties together and brings to life the other truths that Jesus proclaimed.

Personal Calling, Disciple Making, and Activism

Church historians and scholars highlight that every Christian has at least two callings: a primary or common calling and a secondary or unique calling. Throughout all time, all Christians, everywhere, have shared a primary or common calling that unites us through a common cause and mission.

We are to be disciples, who make disciples, wherever we are!

Our secondary callings are unique to each of us. Ephesians 2:10 says that each of us is uniquely made with specific good works and deeds to accomplish. Jesus gives us these callings so that we can directly participate in the mission He has for us—to carry His fullness to others into every crack and cranny of society.

In my book, *More: Find Your Personal Calling and Live Life to the Fullest Measure*[2], I address the vital importance of keeping our unique secondary callings (including our passions and burdens that drive our personal activism) aligned to our primary calling to be disciples who make disciples.

We need to mobilize followers of Jesus on their secondary calling. But we should always keep the perspective that He gives us our secondary callings (passions, burdens, gifts, etc.) to fulfill our primary calling. If I focus on growing the fullness of Jesus in me and intentionally seek to carry that fullness to others as I make disciples, my secondary callings will uniquely position me for engaging those in my unique mission field. I have to learn to properly contextualize my unique calling and burden with His core cause and purpose.

Our challenge is to keep His main thing (disciple making) our main thing. We can simultaneously live out our secondary callings or causes as activists for our unique calling. However, if we focus primarily on our unique activist cause —elevating it above Jesus's primary one—we won't get the results He intends. At that point, we lose sight of the purpose that Jesus uniquely equipped us for, as well as His purpose for giving us passions and burdens. When this happens, we live a form of idolatry. But if we focus on biblical disciple making as our primary cause, we'll mobilize an army of Christ followers who will change the world as they champion a myriad of secondary causes and burdens.

Puritan Minister Cotton Mather used a great metaphor to describe the consequences of elevating our secondary callings (our activist pursuits) above our primary calling to be disciples who make disciples. Mather describes a rowboat propelled by two oars. One oar represents our primary calling and the other oar our secondary calling. Put no oars in the water, and you drift with the winds of culture. Put only one oar in the water, and you spin in circles. When our secondary calling takes priority over our primary calling, it's like having one oar in the water. No matter how loud we trumpet the message of our cause, we just spin in circles. We progress forward only when we put both oars in the water.

As Multipliers, let's commit to keeping Jesus' main thing our main thing. Let's leverage our unique gifts and calling to be activists for good. But let's also position our activism so that our primary fruits produce a movement of biblical disciple makers. In doing so, we'll unleash a movement of love and transformation on the world!

What are the keys to seeing that kind of movement? Multiplication begins and ends with obedient leaders that focus on making disciple makers AND releasing them into the world!

Putting It into Practice

• *Is biblical disciple making the core that drives what you do as a church leader and how you do everything you do? If not, identify what's driving your words and actions.*

• *Other than disciple making, what are some things you try to use as a foundation for multiplication?*

• *If we don't have a solid biblical foundation, why does our activism become idolatry?*

• *Is disciple making one of your strengths? Are you leading your church to make biblical disciples or cultural Christians?*

• *We often hijack Jesus' intended method of adding and making disciples. How do we do this? What are the consequences?*

• *How are you doing personally at making disciple makers? Find out at http://church-multiplication.com/disciplemaker/. This FREE online assessment takes only 20 minutes to complete, and you get your results immediately.*

exponential.org

Chapter 4
Obedience

Be fruitful and increase in number; multiply on the earth and increase upon it.
~ God

In Genesis chapter 1, God speaks to man for the first time. The first words of our Creator to those He has created in His own image are… "be fruitful and multiply." We see God give the same command a few chapters later in Genesis chapter 9 when after forty days of devastating rain, God's first commandment to Noah is: "Be fruitful and increase in number; multiply on the earth and increase upon it" (Gen. 9:7).

Clearly, fruitfulness and multiplication are important to God! But how does healthy increase happen?

Local Addition and Global Multiplication

First, it's reasonable for us to conclude that these increases come through some combination of addition and multiplication. In the context of God's command, the increase rests on our understanding of addition. Second, it's also reasonable for us to conclude that the family unit was God's design and plan for populating the earth. The family unit provides the mechanism for "increase" through reproduction and the union of a husband and wife.

Look at what God did *not* command and what did *not* happen as He repopulated the earth. God did not say to Noah, "I will give you 6,000 years of life to grow one huge family with billions of children." Instead, God established a micro or local strategy via the family where children would be "added" to individual families. Those children would develop, mature, and eventually be released and sent to establish families of their own. From one family to three to nine to twenty-seven to eighty and beyond.

Multiplication spreads far and wide while addition accumulates tall and narrow.

Consider my family and how three generations have added AND multiplied. My grandparents (first generation) added 5 children to their family (including my dad). Those five children married, resulting in a total of 6 family units (grandparents plus their 5 kids) after just one generation. Those five children then added 13 more children to their families. Those 13 married, resulting in 19 total family units after just the second generation. The 13 children of the second generation have now added over 20 more children to their families. Assuming those 20 marry, that will produce over 40 family units after just three generations. My grandparents added 5. Those 5 have multiplied to 40.

The micro or local strategy for increase is addition within the family unit. The macro strategy for increase is multiplication of families to the ends of the earth. Each multiplication of a family provides a new context for the addition of individuals who can then become the fuel for additional new families in the future.

This is addition AND multiplication the way God naturally designs it. It's the way the church is intended to function. It should be so simple. Unfortunately, our accumulation growth strategies and scorecards get in the way. Most churches behave as if they must make the biggest impact possible through addition and accumulation in a single, prolonged generation, never releasing and sending children to start additional churches.

Let's look at a second example of healthy growth. Jesus spent three years discipling twelve men. These men were his spiritual family. He showed them a powerful addition strategy for adding the "next one." Life-on-life discipleship living in community together. He then activated His Church as the basic context for addition. Just as the family unit provides a powerful mechanism for adding new children, the Church functions in a similar way, sending disciples to multiply new churches.

Jesus commanded His disciples to, "Go and make disciples of all nations":

"You will be my witnesses in Jerusalem, and in all Judea and Samaria,
and to the ends of the earth."

Look at what Jesus did *not* say and what the disciples did *not* do as His witnesses to the ends of the earth. Jesus did not say, "Stay in Jerusalem and build an ever-enlarging church." Nor did He say, "Focus most of your energy on accumulating." Instead, He commissioned us to "make disciples," His micro or local strategy happening wherever the Church is. But He also said, "Go to the ends of the earth as you do it." That is a macro multiplication strategy. To stay in Jerusalem and build a bigger and bigger church would have been an addition strategy that replaced multiplication. Jesus intends for us to have a local addition strategy AND a global multiplication reach.

In this context, Jesus' strategy for increase is addition through discipleship at the local level within the church. His plan for multiplication to the ends of the earth is by starting new "faith families" to the ends of the earth. Just like each multiplication of a family provides a new context for the addition of individuals (the family strategy given to Noah), each multiplication of a church provides a new context for addition via disciple making at the local level. There is a powerful synergy between addition and multiplication strategies.

How we respond to and embrace Jesus' addition AND multiplication design becomes a significant factor in shaping the growth culture we develop in our churches. It also influences how we develop as leaders.

The Pursuit of Accumulation

Before Israel ever had a king, God warned His people that future kings would be susceptible to sinful accumulation motives that would distract them and hinder their obedience to God. In Deuteronomy 17:14-20, God commanded the following through Moses:

> *"When you enter the land the LORD your God is giving you and have taken possession of it and settled in it, and you say, 'Let us set a king over us like all the nations around us,' be sure to appoint over you a king the LORD your God chooses. He must be from among your fellow Israelites. Do not place a foreigner over you, one who is not an Israelite. The king, moreover, must not acquire great numbers of horses for himself or make the people return to Egypt to get more of them, for the LORD has told you, 'You are not to go back that way again.' He must not take many wives, or his heart will be led astray. He must not accumulate large amounts of silver and gold."*

Of all the things God could have preemptively demanded of His future kings, He chose to single out the pursuit of "accumulation." Why? We see the answer in the above verses. When a leader's scorecard is rooted in accumulation, he will take his eyes off God and obedience to His commands. Our focus on accumulating more easily becomes a form of idolatry, rooted in the wrong motives. God warns His people that their leaders should instead focus on obedience and faithfulness to God.

Jesus Himself confronted the sin of accumulation, saying, "Do not store up for yourselves treasures on earth, where moths and vermin destroy, and where thieves break in and steal. But store up for yourselves treasures in heaven, where moths and vermin do not destroy, and where thieves do not break in and steal. For where your treasure is, there your heart will be also" (Matt. 6:19-21).

By deploying and mobilizing what we have here on earth, we store up treasures in Heaven. Jesus doesn't mince words when He tells us that a focus on accumulation here on earth is an indication of a heart problem that could be rooted in wrong motives.

So, what would it look like if Jesus' way for the Church were exclusively addition-focused? In that scenario, the local church would grow through the addition of disciples. As these disciples learned to trust and obey Jesus and become more like Him, the church would accumulate and use these mature disciples to grow the church larger and larger, rather than releasing and sending these disciples to start new churches. The church would become an unmanageable "come to us" enterprise unable to fulfill its mission to carry the fullness of Jesus into every corner of society. A church that big could never get into the small spaces. It would become inwardly focused, always looking for the best strategy to conquer the next growth barrier.

Instead of creating new capacity for disciple making via new churches, the resources would disproportionately be used to support the internal structures of ever-enlarging existing churches. It would be like Noah rarely sending out his children to start families of their own, opting instead to repopulate primarily through his own efforts.

See the problem? When our scorecards focus primarily on accumulating and adding rather than releasing and sending, as leaders we become focused on addition growth versus multiplication growth.

As we look at multiplication and champion the increase in radically multiplying churches, I want to be clear here that this conversation is not anti-growth. A multiplication-growth culture requires addition at its core. Multiplying churches grow. In fact, the cumulative attendance of multiplying churches and their daughter churches is almost always greater than the attendance at one single, accumulation-focused church. We must build a solid foundation on addition growth at the local church level, but not stop there!

Obedience and Multiplication

Consider God's command to Adam and Noah to "be fruitful and multiply." Then, add in God's promise to Abraham, "I will surely bless you, and I will surely multiply your offspring as the stars of heaven and as the sand that is on the seashore" (Gen. 22:17). In each of these examples, what causes the fruitfulness and multiplication? Did Adam, Noah or Abraham need some master strategy? Intelligence? Money? Fame? No. They were fruitful and multiplied because they obeyed. In other words, the fruit of their obedience was multiplication.

There is no theology of multiplication. There is only a call to surrender to the Lordship of Jesus and to live obediently to His commands. Multiplication is simply the overflow and outcome of our faithfulness to obey Jesus. To focus on producing multiplication without first living in obedience to Him is futile.

Throughout the New Testament, multiplication is the overflow of obedience to Jesus. Consider the feeding of the 5,000. At what point were the loaves and fishes multiplied? Jesus first commanded the disciples to pass out the food. When the disciples acted in obedience to the Master, He supplied the provision for not only them, but also for the whole countryside of hungry people. How about Jesus' parable of the talents? When did the multiplication occur? Only after the servant obeyed his master's command.

We see the same effect in Acts 2, as we read of the faithful and obedient behaviors of the early church. Their reward? We are called to obedience, and God does the multiplying.

"And the Lord added to their number daily!" (Acts 2:47).

"I planted the seed, Apollos watered it, but God has been making it grow" (1 Cor. 3:6).

44

Ultimately, the Great Commission in Matthew 28 is our response to God's commands to multiply and His promises. Pause now and reread the Great Commission through the lens of fruitfulness and multiplication. Just as God gave the command to multiply to Adam and Noah, Jesus gives us the ultimate command to be fruitful. Even better, He tells us how to make it happen.

As, we must wrestle with the question, "Why isn't multiplication happening?" Given the clarity of Jesus' command, why do we so easily embrace accumulation scorecards that suppress both the "disciple-making" and "go" dimensions of the Great Commission?

Disciple Making Isn't Enough!

Without an unwavering resolve to carry out Jesus' Great Commission, we have no hope for healthy church multiplication. We can programmatically start more churches, but if disciple making isn't at our core, we will always fall short of the movements we pray for. We certainly won't move the needle on our "4-10" mission, from less than 4 percent of U.S. churches ever reproducing to greater than 10 percent.

Healthy multiplication that advances the Kingdom requires us to carry out Jesus' command to make disciples by adding AND multiplying. Now, here's the next AND. We are to make disciples AND we are to go! If our disciple-making efforts don't lead to multiplication in the form of starting new communities of faith, then what does that tell us about the health of our efforts? The "go" in Jesus' Great Commission is inseparable from the multiplication of new churches. *Disciple making isn't enough if it doesn't produce the "go."*

If we focus on disciple making, but then accumulate disciples without releasing and sending them, we fall short of obedience to Jesus' command. I wish God had included a longer list of things in Deuteronomy 17 for kings to avoid accumulating. If God were writing the list to church leaders today, what characteristics of our

45

accumulation growth cultures would He include? How would He address our bias to neutering the Great Commission commandment to fuel our accumulation scorecards?

The fruit of healthy, biblical, disciple making must be the "go" impulse of multiplication. To more fully capture the sending or "go" impulse of our Founder's command, we could say: *Disciples who make disciples that plant churches that plant churches that make disciples who make disciples...[and the multiplication chain continues].*

Yes, disciple making is non-negotiable, but we must value and prioritize multiplication as its fruit. To focus exclusively on disciple making without leading people to multiply and "go" is a form of church idolatry. When that happens, we produce churches constrained to Level 3 addition that never reproduce. Simply put, to multiply we must be as intentional about making biblical disciples as we are about making converts, and then we must release and send them to fulfill our Founder's command to "go."

I can't help but think that our churches and our world would look tremendously different if the disciples we made took the Great Commission to make disciples AND to "go" more seriously.

What culture are you creating? Are you making and accumulating disciples, or are you making and releasing disciples? Is your growth addition or multiplication? To answer these questions, check out some basic multiplication concepts in the next chapter as you continue on the path to becoming a Level 5 Multiplier.

Putting It Into Practice

• *Why has Jesus commanded us to have a local addition strategy AND a global multiplication reach? How do the two working together produce healthy multiplication?*

• *Explain the difference between adding disciples and making disciples? How do the two work in harmony in Jesus' way of disciple making?*

• *Why is it not enough to make disciples?*

• *What happens when we only make disciples?*

• *Would you say you're releasing and sending out the disciples you make to birth new communities of faith? If yes, what evidence can you show to that effect? If no, what is keeping you from sending and releasing?*

exponential.org

Chapter 5
Multiplication

You get to decide what legacy you will leave.
~ C.S. Lewis

Apart from a good Sunday head count and offering, most of the pastors I've met dislike and shy away from math. As someone who has spent much of my life surrounded by numbers and physics (in my past life I was a nuclear engineer working with submarines for the U.S. Navy), I find it difficult to address the subject of multiplication without at least touching on some very fundamental concepts of math.

When it comes to church growth and church multiplication, words like "growth," "subtraction," "plateau," "addition," "reproduction," and "multiplication" are unavoidable (remember that we used these words to define the five levels of church cultures in chapter 1).

As leaders, we tend to adopt our own definitions based on our unique context for church. Our temptation might be to look at our success and incorrectly conclude that we're being obedient to Jesus' commands and multiplying. Or to look at our church size and mistakenly conclude that we can't be a reproducing or multiplying church if we're small.

Let's start with a very simple and basic review of some mathematical concepts—just enough basics to equip you for the journey to becoming a Level 5 Multiplier. Rather than making up our own definitions, I'm embracing the terms that have been handed down to us through mathematics. These are not "secular or business" concepts but rather the principles that emerge from God's creation.

Growth
The process of increasing in size. Growth can happen through addition, reproduction, or multiplication. Regardless of the strategy, model, or culture we embrace and pursue, growth is a

primary goal. Level 5 Multipliers must throw off the shackles of an addition-growth scorecard, opting instead for the pursuit of multiplication growth.

Subtraction

The output result (the number of whatever you're seeking to measure) decreases with time. Every positive unit of effort results in a loss or "subtraction" in the output number.

We all know the pain of seasons of subtraction and loss. On the personal front, it might be losing loved ones. In ministry, losing launch team members is agonizing. Subtraction compels us to action. But subtraction is a normal part of life, including the life of a church. Think about the first 500 churches founded in the first century. All (100 percent) of the early churches ultimately experienced subtraction, all the way to their death. But the Church is still around and vibrant today. Not because of the growth of churches, but rather because of the *sending nature* of churches.

As hard as it is to accept and unless God changes the way He has worked in His church for 2,000 years, *any* church that experiences growth will ultimately experience subtraction. It's as certain as death. Churches are born and will eventually die (including yours). Subtraction is inevitable. Embrace it. The reality is that subtraction will likely be the final chapter in whatever church you lead (or start).

Don't let that reality discourage you, but do let it mess with your thinking. In all the turmoil of subtraction, we desperately pursue and seek out addition growth. But addition is temporary. Multiplication, however, carries the legacy of your church to future generations, far beyond the accumulation you achieve in your local context. That's why sending out leaders to multiply and start new churches, and then continuing the movement into the future is so vitally important. Your sending capacity is your best asset, and your sending results could ultimately be your primary legacy.

Plateau

When a church is plateaued, the number of whatever is being measured remains steady over time. Each increment effort seems to produce no discernable increase in the thing being measured. What you add is offset by what you lose. You break even. Some behavioral experts would argue that most things do not remain plateaued over extended periods of time, but tend to be transitional, meaning that either subtraction or addition is likely to emerge from seasons of plateau.

Addition

The number of whatever is being measured increases with time. "Up and to the right" is the measure of success. We instinctively want to see our effort produce fruit. For most of us, results are an inherent motivator. With addition, we see tangible results for our efforts. The harder we work, the more fruitful the results appear to be.

Bill Hybels, founder and senior pastor of Willow Creek Community Church and the Global Leadership Summit, once told me that it gets harder and harder each year at the Leadership Summit to produce the same incremental increase in output quality. In other words, the "up and to the right curve" always wants to taper off to a lower level of production.

To sustain addition growth, we must continually look for new and innovative ways to overcome growth obstacles. New programs, new buildings, cool community centers, great marketing campaigns, new sites, the best worship in town, etc., are all input fuel for output results.

Reproducing

Reproduction is a catalyst or mechanism for addition growth. It's God's natural or organic design for addition growth. We are guaranteed to add when we reproduce. One becomes two (or two become three). It's the natural way families are built and the way God has designed the Church to function. We are to reproduce at all levels: disciples, artists, leaders, church planters, churches, etc.

When we embed reproduction in our DNA and sustain it in our practices and behaviors, we get multiplication. You might say that reproduction is the natural building block from addition to multiplication.

Multiplication
A more rapid form of addition: 1 increases to 2 then to 4 then to 8 and so on. Multiplication produces a steeper rise in output for a given level of effort. For example, a couple having twins gets double the output for the same initiating effort. Now imagine the impact to world population if children were always birthed as pairs! You might say that multiplication is "extreme or radical addition" (e.g., Acts 2:47: "… and God added about 3,000 to their numbers that day"). We instinctively love multiplication because the results of our efforts are more visibly fruitful.

Exponential (radical multiplication and movements)
The phenomenon that occurs when multiplication hits a tipping point and becomes self-sustaining, even explosive, in its sustained outputs. Exponential multiplication and movements ebb and flow and don't typically sustain themselves indefinitely. You might define "exponential" as exhibiting accelerating multiplication (or rapidly increasing multiplication and thus, "radical multiplication").

Multiplier
An accelerator of results. From 1 to 2 to 4 to 8 to 16 to 32 represents a 2x (or "2 times" multiplier). With each successive cycle, the output increases by a factor of two times. Likewise, from 1 to 10 to 100 to 1,000 represents a 10x (or "10 times" multiplier). Addition-focused scorecards and cultures, however, constrain us to less abundant thinking that moves from 1 to 2 to 3 to 4, and so on. By embracing accumulation cultures, we miss the abundance Jesus intends for us through multiplication.

The best multipliers are leaders like you who surrender their personal addition-based scorecards to a far better scorecard using Jesus' math.

Growth Barriers and Asymptote

Let me introduce one last mathematical concept to help tie together several things in contrasting addition growth with multiplication growth. In nature, things don't naturally continue in a perpetual state of motion without resistance. A rolling ball eventually stops due to the friction it experiences with the ground, and an athlete loses his or her stamina with time. In a similar way, you don't steam through each successive church growth barrier with progressively easier effort. To the contrary, each growth barrier gets more difficult to conquer as you get closer to its summit. This physical phenomenon in nature is called "asymptotes."

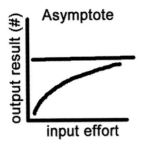

An "asymptote" is like a limit or barrier. In the graph, notice that the start of the curve appears up and to the right like most addition curves. However, with each additional applied effort, the output appears to "slow" or become slightly less than the previous increment. As time goes on, the output results appear to become constrained by and approach the asymptote. In nature, the "asymptote" (represented by the horizontal line in the graph) physically acts like a buffer or limit to suppress the output.

In a church context, this physical phenomenon explains why church leaders and growth experts often say, "there are a number of well-known natural growth barriers at 120, 200, 500, 800, 2,000, etc." In other words, what got us to where we are is not going to get us to where we need to go. To break the 500 barrier, we can't act like we did when we had 40 people. We need to change what we do to break through the current asymptote. Unfortunately, another asymptote a little higher up on the growth curve will be waiting for us.

This progression of conquered hills is also leaving a growing number of pastors questioning whether they've "put their ladder against the right wall": *What if we climb the ladder of addition-growth success only to realize someday that we've had our ladder against the wrong wall?*

I still remember the first cohort of leaders in our Future Travelers initiative when Senior Pastor Steve Andrews said to the group, "I planted my church, and God grew it big. We've done externally focused, church planting, and multisite, and we'll keep doing them. But there are not enough years left in my life to simply keep growing this thing bigger. I'm interested in something more viral. I'm interested in changing the conversation from 'where is our next one?' to 'how do we release 250 of our members to take our city?'"

This continual challenge and struggle to conquer the next growth barrier can trap churches in an addition-constrained culture, keeping them from ever focusing on multiplication. Churches stuck in this endless game are never satisfied and never win, all the while remaining distracted from experiencing the more satisfying multiplication culture. Growth will always yield at least addition (and vice versa), but growth does not always produce multiplication. Thus, we can become satisfied with addition growth but fall far short of experiencing multiplication growth. Addition growth is good, but multiplication growth is even better.

The telling question we want to pose to Multipliers (regardless of context) comes down to what *type* of growth you're pursuing or experiencing. Addition or multiplication? Possibly without consciously knowing it, you've embraced or have at least been captivated by an addition-growth scorecard for your measure of success.

Pause and think again about the culture you're creating. If God answered all your prayers today and solved the church tensions you face and struggles that get you down, which mathematical result discussed above (subtraction, plateau, addition, reproduction or multiplication) would blossom into full bloom? Be honest. You probably want to say "multiplication," but at this point you can't.

It's highly likely your scorecard for success is the best of the addition-growth paradigm. It's the prevailing scorecard we've embraced, and that has become part of our paradigm for success.

Multipliers throw off the captivity of addition-growth scorecards, opting instead to pursue multiplication and eternal legacy. But before you can pursue change in your church, you must take a good look at your personal scorecard!

Putting It into Practice

• *How are you currently (or in the past) working to sustain addition-growth? What new initiatives, ideas or programs are you pursuing to keep your church growing?*

• *What type of growth are you pursuing or experiencing? Addition or multiplication?*

• *Do you agree that your sending capacity is your church's greatest asset? Why or why not?*

• *In what ways have you embraced accumulation and missed the abundance Jesus intends for us through multiplication?*

• *How has the ongoing challenge to conquer the next growth barrier kept you captive in a culture focused on accumulation?*

exponential.org

Chapter 6
Scorecards

"Search me, God, and know my heart; test me and know my anxious thoughts. See if there is any offensive way in me..." (Psalm 139:23-24).

I've never been a hockey fan. The long list of reasons is rooted in my inability to logically follow the game (if a "game" is what you call an encounter between two hockey teams). The puck is too small for my eyes to follow on television, and the rules are so confusing that I've given up trying to understand what "off sides" and "icing" even mean. However, despite these barriers, I do understand the universal language of what it means to win.

The team with the most points at the end of the game wins, every time. I don't need special training to understand that. The purpose of a hockey match is clear. Score the most points! After watching the first 58 minutes of the 2017 Stanley Cup championship game, I instinctively understood the significance of a "0-0" tie score with only two minutes left in the game. While the first 58 minutes were entertaining for some, all that would matter in the next two minutes was which team scored the winning goal!

Our scorecards inherently reflect the purpose of the game. Baseball? Score the most runs. Golf? Hit the ball the fewest number of times. Swimming? Complete the fastest laps. This may sound obvious, but champions ALWAYS understand the right measure for winning and use the scorecard to drive their success.

Wrong Metrics and False Summits

If we surveyed churches asking them for a single scorecard metric that reflects their purpose and how they measure success, we'd get a wide range of answers. Some leaders would say "baptisms," some, "new believers or converts," and yet others, "life transformation." All are important metrics, but they're not the purpose of the Church. You can lead your church to do all of these things extremely well and still produce cultural Christians as your primary product.

As we discussed in chapter 3, any purpose that we embrace other than making biblical disciples fully surrendered to Jesus will lead us down the wrong path—likely leading to Level 3 accumulation. Your core scorecard and metric for Level 5 multiplication must be rooted in making biblical disciple makers who make disciples who plant churches that plant churches

We don't see movements, or even multiplication, in the U.S. Church because most leaders embrace the wrong scorecards and measures of success. Think about it. How many biblical disciple makers in our faith community have made disciples who make disciples to the third and fourth generation? Instead of measuring the number of Level 5 disciple makers we produce, we've shifted our focus to more butts, bigger budgets, and bigger buildings. We measure the things that fuel our lust for addition growth and accumulation rather than the disciple makers who fuel multiplication. The largest, fastest-growing, and most innovative church lists represent the trophy that most Level 3 church leaders pursue.

In fact, sometimes what we think are destinations or points of arrival are actually the gateway to new points of departures. The prize at the end of the path we're on can be like a false summit in mountain climbing. We think we're about to arrive at the peak, only to find there is another path to conquer on our elusive pursuit of winning.

The pull to addition-based success is strong. I know I've had times in my life where I've fought the good fight, sacrificed, and persevered, with my eyes on the wrong summit. I'm an adventurer and conqueror, always pulled toward opportunity, and always needing to be a good steward of discerning the "good" from the "great." I'm guessing you can relate. None of us want to look back someday and conclude that we missed opportunities and pursued the wrong things in life.

Church leaders are especially susceptible to pursuing false summits. In fact, the prevailing scorecard for success in the U.S. Church is a false summit. The Level 3 addition-focused scorecard is beautiful and captivating, like the seductress in the Proverbs. But it never fully satisfies and quickly draws us into an elusive pursuit of the next prize.

We can get caught in the search for that "arrival point"—where we can finally do all the things we've seen larger, more "successful" Level 3 churches doing. Hire staff. Build buildings. Create programs. Conduct monster outreach events and marketing campaigns. Add sites and services. Experience some form of financial stability. Implement amazing leadership pipelines and mobilize waves of volunteers to grow. All great things, but often dead-ended. The false summits of Level 3 are interconnected with other false summits and rarely lead to the better Level 5 summit of multiplication.

So, Multipliers, if the Church's prevailing scorecard has been hijacked—focused on the wrong primary outcome—how do we turn things around? How do you courageously make a difference? A commitment to a Level 5 multiplication scorecard is a vital first step. But that's just the start. You must then turn the commitment into action, and that action needs to start first with your own personal scorecard.

This chapter is a difficult one. This conversation is not about your church but rather, *your* heart and your true motives. It will make you uncomfortable. But remember, the first step in overcoming an addiction is acknowledging our weakness and utter helplessness. If we're embracing the wrong scorecards, we must first look inward. Embracing the right personal scorecard will require surrender. Quite possibly, very difficult surrender that requires you to deal with some impure motives and heart conditions.

Be encouraged, however. Many heroes of the faith who have come before you have taken the same courageous and necessary steps to embrace and live out Level 5 multiplication scorecards. Honestly and thoughtfully answering difficult questions will help you get to the core of the motives and heart factors that shape your personal scorecard.

Throughout the rest of this chapter, we're talking about what it means to change your personal scorecard—your own definition of success—and then confront and work through the internal tensions that inevitably come with heart change. Putting a personal scorecard into practice is hard work. This isn't an easy journey by any means, but it is a worthwhile one—a journey that no doubt ends with eternal legacy.

'Search Me Oh God'

This idea of changing your personal scorecard requires a degree of soul-searching that I'm going to guess you've not yet encountered. It's one thing to say your church needs to change and begin to diagnose the failing areas or opportunities for improvement; it's another to pray like the Psalmist David prayed, "Search *me*, God, and know *my* heart; test *me* and know *my* anxious thoughts. See if there is any offensive way in *me*…" (Psalm 139:23-24, emphasis added).

Throughout Scripture, God reveals His passion for our hearts:

Above all else, guard your heart, for everything you do flows from it (Prov. 4:23).

I the Lord search the heart and examine the mind … (Jer. 17:10).

… *for God sees not as man sees, for man looks at the outward appearance, but the LORD looks   at the heart* (1 Sam. 16:7).

Clearly, God cares more about the condition of our hearts than He does about our accomplishments.

In chapter 3 of his Exponential eBook, *Flow: Unleashing a River of Multiplication in Your Church, City and World,* my friend and Level 4 Multiplier Larry Walkemeyer shares his multiplication journey, noting the personal scorecard change that *had* to take place before he could lead his church, Light and Life Fellowship in Long Beach, California, from Level 3 to Level 4 and now Level 4+.

"I had to do a tough and candid assessment of the scorecard that was motivating me to produce results," he writes. "God had to do a work *in* me before He could do a work *through* me. During that process, He revealed several things that needed to change in me to enable the changes that were needed in my church."[1]

As Larry reflected on this deeply personal shift, he tapped into and transparently shared hidden tensions he never saw coming. These tensions almost derailed his multiplication focus. As he says it, personal fears unintentionally built a "play it safe" wall in his life and ministry.

"I wanted to build and live behind a wall that would keep our church safe from any threats to its survival or growth," he writes. "The atmosphere was self-protective selfishness that said, 'We have a good thing going; why risk it by giving some of it away?'"[2]

The Fear Demon

Fear can be personally paralyzing, especially when we're blind to its impact. I'm convinced that fear is a key factor in our bias to embracing the wrong personal scorecards. Throughout Scripture, we read that the battle is not against flesh and blood. God wants us to know that our battle is a spiritual one—against Satan. The demon of fear is real.

Larry transparently shares a list of fears in *Flow* that held him captive to addition-focused scorecards. His candor reveals several fears that are also at play in all of us. Larry gave me permission to share the following list to encourage you in your own journey as a Multiplier. Pay close attention to the end questions in italics and see if you can identify with any of Larry's fears:

The fear of failure—What if we give away leaders, people and money, and then the projects fail? We were winning at addition; why risk losing at multiplication? *What if church planting damaged our mother church? Could we recover?*

The fear of rejection—Larry realized that multiplication meant allowing allegiances to transfer from the "sending pastor" to the "planting pastor." This kind of emotional exchange called for deep personal security. Insecurity is a form of fear, so he faced his own inner fears of rejection. *Was I secure enough in God and in my own identity to face what would feel like a form of abandonment?*

The fear of loss of control—Multiplication is an empowerment of others, a divesting of the direct management of leaders and people. In his journey, Larry asked, "Did I trust God enough to hand over large groups of people to novice shepherds?" He continues to ask that question, acknowledging that surrender is an ongoing, daily process. Each time he plants, he encourages everyone in his church to ask God if they're being called to go. He has no control over who leaves on the mission. *Could I trust God to replace key staff and lay leaders if they left?*

The fear of conflict—Moving forward in multiplication will undoubtedly create significant pushback, or even division, that can be avoided. Everyone loves addition, but many fear multiplication; consequently, it's difficult to cast and pursue this vision without generating sparks. Larry notes that by nature, he's a conflict avoider. Whenever possible, he would naturally delay or detour around confrontation. *Could I deal with the fallout from developing this controversial new priority in our church?*

The fear of change—Larry recalls that what he and Light & Life were doing was working well, but that he also recognized "good" as often the chief enemy of "great." It's scary to change something that seems "good enough" because you want to "wall it in," so that nothing can alter it. However, once he became convicted of the biblical priority of multiplication over addition, the question was not, "What works?" but, "What is obedience?" *How was God calling us to step out in faith?*

For Larry, inner fears were like mooring lines keeping a boat tied to a pier. He could build a bigger boat as long as he didn't have to untie the lines of fear that would let her sail to the world. He knew what it felt like to build the boat, but not what it meant to free her and let the wind of the Spirit take her where He wanted.

The fear of financial hardship—When Larry's team invited large groups of people to take their tithes and offerings and leave with a church plant, he had no idea how much money they were actually talking about. He and his wife, Deb, have watched as much as 25 percent of the church's monthly income flow out to launch a new church. Anticipating this reality made him want to build a wall around their tithers. *Would God really provide all of the finances we needed?*[3]

A special note from Larry: "I've taught the principle of tithing to many people. I always acknowledge that giving to God the first 10 percent you make can be scary if you've never done it. I'm sure you've done that, as well, in your preaching. But I have collected hundreds of stories affirming that when you practice this kind of obedience and generosity, God unleashes blessings in an undeniable manner. If this is true in personal tithing, how much more is it reflected in the giving of people, energy and resources for the work of church multiplication? Every leader would do well to consider how to tithe to the work of multiplication. At Light & Life, once we began to demonstrate our faith that, 'You can't out-give God,' we began to experience His richness in unprecedented ways."[4]

How about you? Be honest. Look inward and identify the fears that have been at work in your life and ministry. The demon of fear may be deep-rooted. Embracing a Level 5 scorecard requires you to do the hard work of identifying the fears that are holding you back and keeping you captive to Level 3 behaviors.

Rank each of the six fears listed above on a 1 to 10 scale (1= no impact; 10 = significant impact). Commit to calling out and naming your fears. Make a journal entry for each one, describing specifically how your past and current context reveals it. Practice bringing your fears into the light of day. Share your list with your spouse and at least one close friend. Pray diligently for God to release you from these fears.

10 Factors Contributing to Wrong Scorecards

As if fear were not enough for us to deal with in overcoming addition lust, each of us also carries biases and sinful behaviors that make us susceptible to pursuing and embracing accumulation-based scorecards. Carefully read through the list of internal tensions below and ask God to reveal any areas you need to address. Please resist the temptation to skim them. Take the time to ask yourself each of these questions and in a "search me, O God" posture, consider each one. Don't be overwhelmed by these questions. Instead, use them as a diagnostic tool to assess the condition of your heart.

1. **Ego:** Is my personal self-image predicated on the size of our church? Am I measuring my personal scorecard for success based on "bodies, budgets and buildings"? Does my zeal to obtain these three B's block my/our church's ability to prioritize multiplication?

2. **Pride:** Do I consider the church "mine" instead of "His"? Does anything that threatens the image of the church threaten my self-image, too?

3. **Trust**: Do I find it difficult to trust God to replenish what I give away? Deep down, do I believe it's more blessed to receive than to give?

4. **Insecurity:** Am I measuring my ability to multiply by my evaluation of other leaders or churches I've watched do it so successfully? Do I ever find myself thinking, *I'm not as good as they are?* Have I seen a church-planting failure and thought, *That will inevitably happen to me, as well*?

5. **Control**: Do I desire to multiply ministries even though I'll have no direct control over them? Is my reluctance to relinquish control actually restricting multiplication?

6. **Hero Complex**: In practice, do I live as though my church's success has more to do with me than with God?

7. **Complacency:** Am I willing to work hard to not only tend to my own flock but also help another church start? The hard work required often diminishes the motivation of multiplication.

8. **Reputation:** Am I seeking out my denomination or network's award or recognition based on attendance and dollars with little regard for multiplication?

9. **Harmony:** Deep down, do I think the battle to sell such a radical vision is worth the fight? Is significant pushback or division tempting me to truncate the vision toward a more self-serving initiative?

10. **Perspective**: Have I been adequately exposed to a multiplication vision or the information I need to instill a priority of a multiplication culture?[5]

While you may have additional internal tensions not on this list (if so, take note of them), this is a good starting place for self-assessment. Just as you did with the previous list of fears, do an inventory of these additional factors in your ministry. Rank each one on a 1 to 10 scale (1 = no impact; 10 = significant impact). Commit to calling out and naming each one in your life. Make a journal entry for each one, describing specifically how your past and your current context reflect this fear. Share your list with your spouse and at least one close friend. Pray diligently for God to release you from these sins.

Redefining Success

It's true that the "speed of a leader shapes the speed of their team." For you, it's also true that the strength of your personal scorecard shapes the strength of your church's scorecard. If you have a Level 3 church scorecard, then you inevitably have a Level 3 personal scorecard! Change starts in the heart and mind of the leader.

The dashboard indicators on the scorecard of a Level 5 multiplying church are relatively straight- forward. Most involve metrics of deployment and multiplication rather than accumulation and growth. They include things like:

-The number of disciple makers who are making disciples to the third generation,
-The number of leaders who know and have been mobilized on their unique calling to carry the fullness of Jesus into every corner of society,
-The transformation occurring in community mission fields embraced by everyday missionaries mobilized from your church
-The number of churches planting churches that you've started.

Only you can decide and act on the specific measures you embrace. But you'll be limited by the nature of your own personal scorecard. Are you positioned to be the hero of your church's story, or are you modeling a life of hero making? Are you a king overseeing the building of an empire, or are you a servant making missionaries of everyday Christians who are God's agents of change in the world? Will you measure success by what you do and accumulate, or by what you deploy and equip others to deploy?

From Scoring to Assisting

I'm reminded of a metaphor that Larry Walkemeyer has developed in his own journey to embracing a Level 5 scorecard. Larry shares a powerful illustration of a leader who multiplies—and the leader God uses. He paints a picture of an NBA basketball game that has drastically changed the rules. In addition to field goals being worth two or three points, every assist (a pass that empowers someone else to score) is worth five points. The impact, he says, would totally alter the game.

What if making assists (hero making) were worth more points than making baskets (being the hero)?

"The celebrity shooters would no longer dominate teams, but the effective passers would be of even greater value," Walkemeyer writes. "High scorers could be those who never even made a shot. Team play would rise to a whole new level, with scores potentially surpassing 250 points.

"I believe God scores the assists. He's searching for 'passers' even more than 'shooters.' He's looking for leaders who are more concerned about who they can launch than how many they can lead. For too long, the scoreboard has been skewed and leaders haven't played up to our Kingdom potential."[6]

How we handle and deal with our internal tensions makes all the difference in how we lead and multiply others. What would happen if church leaders operated in God's economy? If leaders who looked for ways to multiply other leaders wound up scoring more points than the star leaders who feel the need to carry the team? Do you have the right motives and personal scorecard? Any multiplying leader will tell you this is a non-negotiable.

The next question to ask, then, is how do I begin to move toward Level 5 leadership? Keep reading to discover five essential practices for becoming leaders who pass way more than they shoot—Multipliers who lead beyond addition.

Putting It into Practice

• *What are your top three measurements of success as a leader? In other words, what are the most important metrics (which you actually measure) that define your personal scorecard?*

• *Are these metrics primarily about sending/releasing or gathering/accumulating?*

• *Are there human factors (accomplishments, resources, talents, security, etc.) that you've come to rely on more than Jesus?*

• *What is the single biggest internal tension you face in leading beyond addition to multiplication?*

• *How would you rate yourself (1 to 10) as a Level 5 leader?*

Exponential Tools for Becoming Multipliers

Flow: Unleashing a River of Multiplication in Your City, Your Church and World by Larry Walkemeyer Level 4 Multiplier Larry Walkemeyer candidly shares the story of how his Long Beach, California, church shifted from survival to addition to a world-impacting multiplication movement.

Play Thuno: The World-Changing Multiplication Game by Larry Walkemeyer. In this free eBook, Larry gets uber practical, highlighting principles for multiplication, twenty-one leadership essentials for multiplication and even deceptions that often derail our efforts to reproduce. Most significant, however, is Larry's thorough exploration of Scripture to discover *why* churches must multiply.

Chapter 7
Hero Making

My fruit grows on other people's trees.
~Bob Buford

Who doesn't want to be the player who scores 30 points in a basketball game? The hero of the team?

Heroes are celebrated.

Down deep, we each long to live lives bigger than ourselves. We're naturally drawn to the superhero role, putting ourselves at the center of the story. When you watch a movie, my guess is you rarely see yourself in the shoes of the supporting cast.

Being a hero is a good thing. But being a hero maker is a great thing—a role that shifts my focus from addition to multiplication, and from "me" to "others." The shift is counter-cultural. Ultimately, it's a shift that makes me much more like Jesus!

Behind every hero is at least one *hero maker*. We've already introduced this concept (HeroMaker is Exponential's 2018 theme), but in this chapter we're taking a deep dive into what it means to be a hero maker and how we start to shed our "hero" role and become hero makers.

From Hero to Hero Maker

True hero makers die to themselves and are willing to live in the shadows of others, faithfully embracing the role of supporting character. They don't seek to be the central figure in the main plot. Instead, their main plot is to faithfully make heroes who make heroes who make heroes. I think of Barnabas, the hero maker to Paul and others. The scales had barely fallen from Paul's eyes before Barnabas had taken him to the apostles and vouched for him. Later, he took Paul to the Antioch church, ultimately setting him up for planting churches that would advance the cross and change the world. Barnabas shifted from hero to becoming the mentor who creates heroes that ultimately become mentors (for example, Paul to Timothy).

Hero makers have a pattern of continually investing in others to help them be all Jesus intends for them. As my mentor and friend Bob Buford says, "I want to be a cheerleader who gives permission, encouragement, and accountability to release the potential in others."

Of course, Jesus is the ultimate hero maker. Throughout the Gospels, we see hero making consistently lived out in Jesus' life and ministry. His death on the cross was heroic. He stretched out His arms and said, "Not my will, but yours be done" (Luke 22:42). He invested in us, through His death, so that the best of what God intended for us could be redeemed and made whole.

But Jesus didn't stop there. He made heroes out of his closest followers. Jesus was pretty explicit about His desire to equip His followers to do the heroic: "Very truly I tell you, whoever believes in me will do the works I have been doing, and they will do even *greater things* than these because I am going to the Father" (John 14:12, emphasis added). Jesus told the disciples that He was setting them up so that they could reach *more* people, go to *more* places, write a book we call the Bible, and make *more* disciples than He *ever* would during His three years of earthly ministry.

You can't study Jesus' ministry practices without seeing Him as a hero maker, someone who puts the spotlight on others, who in turn do likewise for others. He modeled it in how He lived, calling us to be hero-making Level 5 Multipliers.

While Level 5 leadership requires that we embrace the right personal scorecard and deal with our misplaced personal motives, we can't stop there. God doesn't want us becoming mired in our internal tensions. Instead, we need to move forward and be intentional about practices that will move us from Levels 1-4 to Level 5 leadership.

Level 5 leadership requires that we become hero makers. The personal scorecards of hero makers are measured not by what *they* do, but rather by how they release the potential in others. How can we move from being addition heroes of our story to multiplication HeroMakers for God's glory?

Becoming HeroMakers: 5 Essential Practices

Our 2018 theme book, *Hero Maker: 5 Essential Practices for Leaders to Multiply Leaders* by Dave Ferguson and Warren Bird (Zondervan – available early 2018) takes an in-depth look at what it means to make the shift from being a leader who's focused on "their thing" to a leader who multiplies and empowers others to go out and do "God's thing."

As Dave and Warren sat out to define what a hero maker is, they identified five essential practices we see in the life and ministry of Jesus and in the leadership of every contemporary hero maker. While a hero maker will use these five practices in developing an apprentice, they are also leadership values that will continually show up as leadership values in everything hero makers do.

The following is a preview of the 5 shifts in practice from our 2018 theme HeroMaker:

HeroMaking Practice 1: Multiplication Thinking

The first HeroMaking practice is a shift to multiplication thinking—a shift in *thinking*. You move from thinking the best way to maximize ministry is through your own efforts to understanding that it actually happens through developing the leadership of others. We see this in the life of Jesus in Acts 1:8 when He casts a vision for taking the gospel to the ends of the earth and explains to His followers that He's going to do it through them: "… and you will be my witnesses." Jesus didn't think the mission would happen just though Him during His time on this earth; He knew it would happen through others who would equip others who would equip still others. Jesus practiced multiplication thinking.

HeroMaking Practice 2: Permission Giving

The second HeroMaking practice is permission giving—a shift in *seeing*. You take the focus off your leadership and begin to see the leadership potential in the people all around you. Looking for and identifying leadership potential in the people around you will cause you to begin to lead with a bias to "yes" and give them permission to fully engage in the mission. We see this in the life of Jesus when He says to a group of rag-tag working class fellows, "Come follow Me." They never expected a rabbi to see them as worthy of teaching and leading. But Jesus saw in them a group that could change the world. He not only gave them permission; He also told them they could change the world!

HeroMaking Practice 3: Disciple Multiplying

The third HeroMaking practice is disciple multiplying—a shift in *sharing*. You begin to share not just what you know to help others follow Jesus, but to also share your life and invest in the development of leaders who do the same for other leaders. We see this in the life of Jesus as He spent three years with primarily twelve people. The way Jesus did apprenticeship is best explained by the *koine* Greek word *diatribo* meaning, "to spend time with." Jesus spent time with the twelve and shared His life with them, and they, in turn, multiplied themselves into a movement of Jesus followers.

HeroMaking Practice 4: Gift Activating

The fourth HeroMaking practice is gift activating—a shift in *blessing*. Not only do you ask God to bless the gifts He has given you, but you also ask God to bless the leaders you have developed and send out at the end of their apprenticeship. The most obvious example of this is in Matthew 28. Jesus
turns over the leadership of the movement to His closest followers and tells them, in effect, "I have all authority, and will work through you as you go!" Jesus activated their leadership gifts by giving them His blessing to "go."

HeroMaking Practice 5: Kingdom Building

The last and fifth HeroMaking practice is Kingdom building—a shift in *counting*. You are no longer only concerned with who's showing up at *your* thing; you also count who's doing God's thing! Jesus told His followers in simple terms, "Seek first the Kingdom of God." They followed this admonition, and all that mattered was that God was keeping track of how the Jesus mission was being advanced around the world.

By this point, do you see the huge difference between being a hero and a hero *maker*? The following comparison chart from the authors of *Hero Maker* helps you understand the dramatic contrast:

Practice	Heroic Leadership	HeroMaking Leadership
Multiplication Thinker	I *think* ministry happens through my own leadership.	I *think* ministry happens through multiplied leaders.
Permission Giver	I *see* what God can do through my own leadership.	I *see* what God can do through others, and I let them know what I see in them.
Disciple Multipliers	I *share* what I've learned in ways that grow followers.	I **share** what I've learned in ways that multiply disciples.
Gift Activator	I ask God to **bless** the use of my own gifts.	I ask God to **bless** leaders I'm sending out.
Kingdom Builder	I *count* people who show up to "my thing."	I *count* leaders who go out and do "God's thing."[1]

73

Multipliers are hero makers. When you shift from being simply the hero of your church to helping others become the heroes, you provide the future mentors your church will need on the journey toward Level 5 multiplication. Level 5 Multiplier Ralph Moore is the first to say that multiplication lives and dies on leaders who are willing to pass the baton and empower others to lead.

If you focus on being a hero, you may do some great things on this side of eternity. However, if you focus on becoming a hero maker, you'll see great things happen through the people you invest in and the people they invest in and so on. That's Hero-Making. It's this kind of leadership that will move the needle on church multiplication.

Multipliers are heroes because they aggressively seek to make heroes of others. They've shifted their scorecard from being a hero to becoming a hero maker. They're moving from being a point scorer, to being the very best assist maker they can be.

Over the next few chapters, we'll look at what it takes to lead and manage multiplication as a hero maker.

Putting It into Practice

• *The shift from hero to hero maker starts in the heart of the leader. Why is this internal shift important in multiplication, and what does it look like for you, practically?*

• *What specific practices must you do to implement this hero shift in your leadership?*

• *If you exclusively focused on making this hero-making shift (and no other major initiatives), what actions would you need to take?*

• *What are the benefits and the consequences of full-time paid staff being the "heroes" rather than "hero makers?" How does this impact your church's ability to move to Level 5 multiplication?*

• *Can you identify potential hero-makers in your church? Who are they? Are you releasing them for multiplication or retaining them to grow your church?*

Exponential Tools for Becoming Multipliers

Hero Maker: 5 Essential Practices for Leaders to Multiply Leaders by Dave Ferguson and Warren Bird (Zondervan). Exponential's 2018 anchor book takes an in-depth look at what it means to be a hero maker and explores five essential practices for making the shift from being a leader who's focused on "their thing" to a leader who multiplies and empowers others to go out and do "God's thing."

HeroMaker assessment This free online assessment takes 20 minutes to complete and gives immediate results to help you gauge your effectiveness at becoming a Level 5 HeroMaker. The results give you a solid indication of the scorecard you've embraced and the gap between where you are and becoming a Level 5 Multiplier. Use the assessment with all your leaders as part of your leadership development process.

Chapter 8
Mission

Go and make disciples of all nations, baptizing them in the name of the Father and of the Son and of the Holy Spirit, and teaching them to obey everything I have commanded you (Matt. 28:19-20).
~ Jesus

Known as the father of modern management and author of more than thirty books, Peter Drucker understood the importance of leaders understanding the mission of their organizations. In one of his most powerful (and shortest) books, *The Five Most Important Questions You Will Ever Ask About Your Organization*, Drucker wrote that the first and most important question for leaders is, "What is your mission?" or "What is your core business?" or "Why do you exist?"[1]

"The mission says *why* you do what you do," Drucker explained, "not the means by which you do it."[2]

He was equally passionate that the "how of what you do" naturally flows from a clear and succinct core mission. Drucker, who devoted a great deal of his time to helping church leaders, believed strongly that "the plan begins with a mission," and that a fundamental responsibility of leadership is to make sure everybody knows the mission, understands it, and lives it.

So as Multipliers and hero makers, what is our purpose or mission? I'm hoping you know the answer to that question by now. But it's critical you not only know the answer, but also internalize and personalize it. Ask yourself: *At the end of my life, what do I want to be remembered for—growing a large, Level 3 church or advancing God's Kingdom though a movement of exponentially multiplying churches?*

That question always puts things into perspective for me. As leaders, our mission or purpose is clear (and it meets Drucker's well-known requirement that it fits on a T-shirt): "Disciple making!" or "Making Disciple Makers!" To lead and manage multiplication, you need to look at how multiplication actually happens. We call it 3D Multiplication (3 critical dimensions of multiplication).

Disciple Making: The First Dimension of Multiplication

Ralph Moore knows a thing or two about making disciples. Starting from 12 people in 1971, Moore can now say that the Hope Chapel movement he founded now has ties to more than 2,300 churches planted to date—making it one of the few Level 5 churches in the United States.

"Disciple making is at the heart of Hope Chapel," Moore says, adding that disciple making is his heart, as well. "I'd say that making disciples is 90 percent of this movement. It gives us a solid foundation for a new scorecard that prioritizes Level 5 multiplication over Level 3 addition growth."

Moore shares an early story from his denominational days. Known as the "church-planting guy" in the denomination, he worked hard to convince large churches in the denomination to plant churches.

"They did. They poured resources into these churches—more resources than we had—and most failed. I had gotten everyone in our denomination revved up about planting a church and quickly realized that was the wrong thing to do because these leaders didn't have disciple making as their core. They weren't making disciples. Disciple making is critical to multiplication. At the very beginning, we started discipling people and saw them disciple others."

Think about the huge stadium events Jesus could have filled or the giant megachurch He could have led or the international network He could have handed off to others. But Jesus' command was clear: "Go and make disciples." For three years on earth, He modeled disciple making and made disciple makers. He then commanded them to do the same. When He completed His work here, Jesus told His disciples, "As the father has sent me, I am sending you" (John 20:21). Soon thereafter, He gave His Great Commission to go and make disciples to the ends of the earth.

We can look at disciple making through the lens of adding disciples (making converts) and reproducing (making disciples). The pathways for *adding* disciples—connecting with people, introducing them to Jesus, and bringing them to a point of accepting Him as Lord—are the entry point to making biblical disciples. We add people one follower at a time. Infants in the faith spiritually mature and then reproduce themselves, repeating the cycle.

By making biblical disciples, we become more effective at carrying the fullness of Jesus into every corner of our communities, ultimately sending disciples to *go* (there's that word again) and multiply new churches that create even greater capacity for healthy Kingdom growth. Disciples who make disciples the way Jesus did are the fuel of multiplication movements.

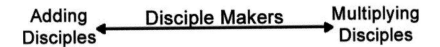

Regardless of our specific strategies, models and approaches, we add people to the movement of Christianity one follower at a time. We can't change that, nor should we try. It's how our Founder designed it to be. Infants in the faith spiritually mature and then reproduce themselves, repeating the cycle. The "adding" and the "making" work together. Those far from God become disciples who give their full devotion to becoming more like Jesus and having His fullness in them. In the process of becoming more mature disciples, they naturally make disciples of others—multiplying themselves in others. Disciples who make disciples the way Jesus did are the fuel of multiplication movements.

Unfortunately, in our addition-oriented growth cultures, we hijack this natural method and create three significant problems.

First, we replace (rather than supplement) Jesus' design for adding disciples (i.e. disciples making disciples) with our man-made growth strategy methods (for example, outreach, marketing, Sunday services, programs, great preaching, etc.). The diagram above showing "Adding Disciples" on one end and "Multiplying Disciples" on the other, fueled by "Disciple Makers," is replaced with a new tension diagram (see below). In the prevailing Level 3 model, we put "Adding Converts (or members)" on one end and "Keeping Cultural Christians Happy" on the other end. That process is fueled by our ever-expanding growth strategies rather than biblical disciple makers who reproduce themselves.

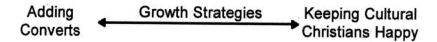

Adding Converts ← **Growth Strategies** → **Keeping Cultural Christians Happy**

Notice that the first tension diagram had addition at one end and multiplication at the other (Adding Disciples versus Multiplying Disciples). Addition/accumulation Level 3 cultures put addition elements at both ends of the tension diagram (e.g., Adding Converts versus Keeping Cultural Christians Happy). When we allow addition elements to define the tension, we unintentionally neuter the multiplication impulse of Jesus' intended approach. We simply create ever-stronger accumulation-based cultures.

Second, many churches struggle with evangelism versus discipleship. Some churches become so focused on corporate pre-evangelism efforts to make converts that disciple making never becomes embedded into their DNA. In fact, disciple making in these churches is disconnected from pre-evangelism activities. You might call it a significant imbalance between evangelism and discipleship versus a balanced and integrated approach. In his free Exponential eBook, *Disciplism*, Alan Hirsch says we need to reframe evangelism within the context of discipleship.

"We must not stop sharing the Good News, but here's the deal: Evangelism gets done along the way as we do discipleship," Hirsch explains. "The Great Commission is just about discipling the nations. Know what happens? As you disciple people, evangelism takes place because it's done in the context of discipleship."[3]

Third, we struggle with the tension between making biblical disciples and cultural Christians. Is it possible that we think we're focusing on Jesus and making biblical disciples when in actuality we're focusing on making cultural Christians? A normal part of the maturation process of biblical disciples is making other disciples. One becomes many. Contrast that with cultural Christians. They consume. Add one and continue having to feed them to keep them happy. When spiritual infants never fully mature and reproduce, cultural Christianity breaks the natural reproduction cycle.

To compensate, we wind up doubling down on our addition-growth strategies (marketing, outreach, programs, etc.). The insanity occurs when we double our efforts to keep adding more to increase our numbers. If our standard is accumulating large numbers of spiritual seekers and cultural Christians without equal diligence to make biblical disciples that make disciples, we will be sorely disappointed in our lack of multiplication.

Disciple making is critical to multiplication and a new Level 5 scorecard! Prioritizing disciple making as your core purpose, both for yourself and for your church, will initiate new conversations and compel you to ask new questions. It will drive new decisions that lead to new and innovative ways of thinking that advances God's Kingdom. That's what hero-making Multipliers do.

Level 5 Disciple Making

Have you ever made something harder than it needed to be? Instead of the simple questions that often give us guardrails and guidance for how we live life and lead our churches, we can choose to focus on the complexities. We miss the easiest path from point A to point B.

For example, when you want your team to do something, you look for the simplest, clearest way to communicate your goal. When my wife wants me to fix something in the house, she doesn't mince words.

Jesus didn't mince words either. He gave us no wiggle room in His command to make and multiply disciples. He was crystal clear! In the simplicity of His strategy, Jesus knows that if we focus on making disciples the way He did and pursue Level 5 disciple making, we will see Level 5 Kingdom multiplication. If we cooperate with Him in this simple strategy, the Holy Spirit will produce the harvest. It's not intended to be complex. Disciples who make disciples in the same way as Jesus—the master disciple maker—are the fuel of Level 5 multiplication movements.

Unfortunately, we don't always hear and embrace the simplicity of His command. Instead of focusing on Level 5 disciple making as our core purpose that drives all of our programming, we tend to align our activities around other motives rooted in accumulation.

Without this first dimension—disciple making that multiplies and produces new communities of faith—we have little hope of moving the multiplication needle. We *won't* see the number of reproducing churches in the United States increase from less than 4 percent to greater than 10 percent. And we'll fall desperately short of Jesus' call. When we don't see new disciple-making churches birthed, we limit our future capacity for disciple making.

As we were finishing up our Disciple Maker's Assessment tool (see becomingfive.org) with discipleship.org, an unexpected result emerged from the two hundred-plus leaders who took the final beta test. Less than one in four leaders (25 percent) aspired to Level 5 disciple making. We thought that number would certainly be greater than 75 percent. Instead, most leaders aspired to Level 4 instead of 5. The difference? Level 4 focuses on making *disciples*. Level 5 focuses on making *disciple makers*. The difference is subtle and yet so profound, representing the catalytic difference between addition growth and more rapid multiplication.

Multipliers, it's vitally important that you embrace a core mission to make disciple makers! Anything less will produce Level 3 accumulation with a continual need to feed cultural Christians.

Capacity Building: The Second Dimension of Multiplication

By making biblical disciples, we become more effective at carrying the fullness of Jesus into every corner of our communities, ultimately sending disciples to go and multiply new churches that create even greater capacity for healthy Kingdom growth. Making cultural Christians also scales our efforts— unfortunately with sideways energy that shunts our multiplication capacity.

As critical as disciple making is to multiplication, on its own it does not guarantee multiplication. As a leader, you're also responsible for building the infrastructure or capacity necessary to expand and support your church's disciple-making context.

Capacity is a physical characteristic that enables future growth. Consider the bones in our bodies. They increase in size as you grow. It takes larger bones to support a larger body. Our bones are one key element of how the body naturally builds capacity to support future growth. The larger our bones, the more size and weight we can support.

Every church (and organization) builds capacity. It's natural. However, the key question is, "What type of capacity are we building?"

Think about how Jesus spent three years building the core capacity for the greatest movement in history. By embedding the gospel DNA for disciple making into twelve followers surrendered to His Lordship, He built capacity. Those leaders passed along the genetic code to others who did the same for others in their path. The right capacity for the right motives built into a small band of believers can change the world.

Have you ever thought that every believer in a church has the capacity for a multiplication movement? Do you grasp that profound truth? In His wisdom, God gave us the Church—in part because we're designed to function like a family, and also to provide us with a platform of capacity for 1) increasing our effectiveness in disciple making, and 2) scaling or multiplying our efforts at disciple making (beyond what unaffiliated, lone ranger disciples can do when they're separated from biblical fellowship).

The institutional part of church, including its infrastructure, processes and resources, is vital to multiplying and sustaining a church's growth via disciple making.

Addition AND Multiplication Capacity

Although multiplication is built on a healthy foundation of addition, we get into trouble when we focus exclusively (or primarily) on addition capacity, neglecting or limiting multiplication capacity. As you read through the rest of this chapter, pay close attention to the balancing act necessary for managing addition and multiplication factors.

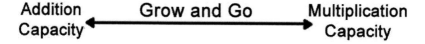

Addition capacity represents everything you do to build and grow your church and impact a local geographic area. Multiplication capacity represents everything you do to make biblical disciples beyond your church.

Think about all of the activities a church can do to create local capacity for adding numbers locally (regardless of the activity's effectiveness at producing biblical disciples). The list includes but isn't limited to adding new worships services, new facilities, new staff, new programs, new sites, marketing, outreach, leadership development systems, etc.

Yes, local capacity is vital to healthy growth. There's nothing wrong with initiating or participating in any of these activities. These activities build a solid base for expanding your multiplication activities. But possibly the single-largest obstacle to multiplication occurs when we position addition-capacity activities as our primary strategy for growth, rather than seeing them as a supporting element to healthy disciple making. Maybe you've experienced that in your church or a church you were part of previously.

Many Level 3 leaders have unintentionally put addition capacity and strategies as the target of their growth efforts. In doing so, they've increased their effectiveness at breaking growth barriers and adding to their numbers, but the unfortunate consequence is that they may simply be building bigger and bigger holding tanks for cultural Christians.

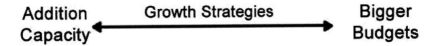

Addition Capacity ←— Growth Strategies —→ **Bigger Budgets**

Often our focus on building addition capacity goes hand in hand with bigger budgets. One feeds the other in a vicious cycle. Once again, when we allow two addition elements to define the tensions we face, we produce stronger accumulation cultures and suppress multiplication.

In the words of C.S. Lewis: "There exists in every church something that sooner or later works against the very purpose for which it came into existence. So we must strive very hard, by the grace of God to keep the church focused on the mission that Christ originally gave to it."[4]

Though we do need it, addition capacity is not the most leveraged form of capacity building. The process of building multiplication capacity creates Kingdom capacity for implementing new environments and contexts for biblical disciple making. This key element requires that we release and send leaders, dollars, and support to start new communities of faith that are not directly under our control and authority.

Think about it this way: Where addition capacity focuses on increasing the capacity to grow trees in your own orchard, multiplication capacity focuses on planting new orchards. We need both. Addition systems and activities enhance healthy multiplication. For example, we can use the same leadership development systems that support local church capacity expansion to develop and deploy church planters.

But we can't be content with just making and adding disciples. We must focus on making disciples of people who will then focus on making disciples of others. And the fruit of disciples making disciples *must* produce leaders who are mobilized to carry the fullness of Jesus into every corner of society. That's the fuel of multiplication.

In the next chapter, we look at the critical element of mobilization and how, working together with the first dimension of multiplication (biblical disciple making) and the second dimension (capacity building), this third dimension completes the 3D Multiplication model.

Putting It into Practice

• *Why is biblical disciple making considered the non-negotiable, essential ingredient in Level 5 leadership?*

• *Is disciple making one of your strengths? Are you leading your church to make biblical disciples or cultural Christians?*

• *We often hijack Jesus' intended method of adding and making disciples. How do we do this? What are the consequences?*
• *How would you define "capacity"? Why is capacity—the second dimension of multiplication—vital to becoming a leader who multiplies?*

• *In what ways are you, as a leader, focusing on building addition-growth capacity? In what ways are you building multiplication capacity?*

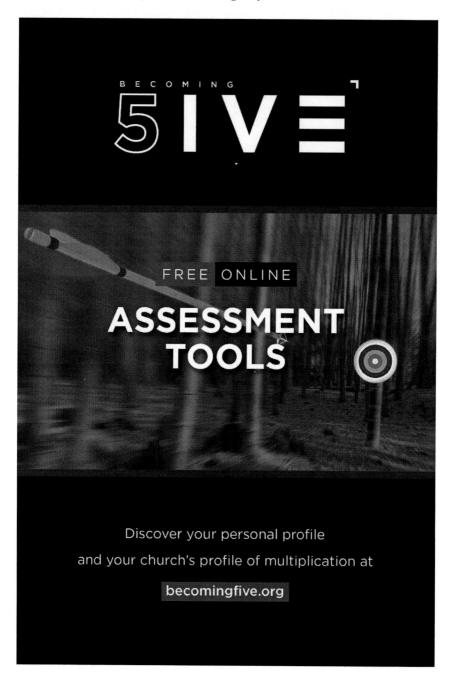

Chapter 9
Mobilization

"As the Father has sent me, even so I am sending you" (John 20:21).

It's easy to miss the power of Jesus' words in this single verse—Jesus, the sent one, revealing to His followers an even bigger calling than they'd first understood. A mission extending beyond the relational warmth of their small group. A cause without the safety and security of their Master in bodily form.

Just a few days earlier before Jesus appeared to His disciples and followers, this band of Jesus freaks had hidden themselves away behind locked doors, grieving the loss of their Founder, unable to see any forthcoming movement. Now Jesus was standing in front of them, giving them their new marching orders.

Jesus knew the disciples' tendency might be to stay together and accumulate. He proactively addressed their bias (and ours). His words are deliberate and intentional. The question is not, *are we sent* but rather *to where and to whom are we sent?* For most of us, the answer lies directly in the mission field already embedded in our lives. The real challenge for the disciples, and for us, is to think and to see through a different paradigm and lens than we've become comfortable with.

Could it be that we spend so much time and energy on attracting and accumulating that we've either forgotten or don't take seriously Jesus' call to "live sent" to the world around us? If Jesus appeared to you and your church this week in bodily form and confronted you with His words—"As the Father has sent me, I am sending you"—what would you change? What would you do differently? Would you try to rationalize that all the accumulating and attracting is somehow acting in obedience to Jesus' command to go?

The desire of the Father's heart is that we are to multiply. It's why He sent His Son. We see it in Jesus' words in John 20 and Matthew 28.

Mobilizing Disciples to Make Disciples: The Third Dimension

As a Multiplier, your role is to simultaneously manage the tensions in these first two dimensions of multiplication: disciple making and building capacity for disciple making. You might say you need the genius of the *"and"* in both disciple making *and* capacity building!

But these two key dimensions are not enough to fulfill Jesus' command to "go." We must also *mobilize* disciples to carry the fullness of Jesus into every corner of society as they make disciples. We must have a culture of empowerment where the fruit of mature disciple making is disciples who *go*.

In his letter to the church in Ephesus, Paul connects the dots for us, showing us how we fit into the disciple-making mission of the Church. In the opening chapter, he offers a great description of the potential of the Church, essentially saying that we (the Church) have the capacity to carry (or to be) the fullness of Jesus into every crack and cranny of society. In the second chapter, he tells us that we are each a unique creation with a specific role to play in carrying the fullness of Jesus to society. And in the fourth chapter, Paul notes that Jesus Himself has equipped each of us with specific gifts to play our unique roles in the mission. To fulfill our mission, we must *mobilize* and *go*!

But mobilization gives us two simultaneous tensions to manage. Scripture calls us to "live in common" as a family of believers via the church community *and* to simultaneously "live deployed" as missionaries in our unique corners of society.

Living in Common ←——— **Everyday Missionary** ———→ **Living Deployed**

As I did research for my book, *More*, I learned that church historians look at personal calling through two lenses. The first is what they call "common" or general calling. We share this calling with all Christians. For example, Jesus has called us to be disciples who make disciples wherever we are. We are also to be healthy functioning children in God's family via the church community. Like the church in Acts 2, we are to "live in common." Look at the collective "they" statements we find in Acts 2:

They met daily.
They broke bread together.
They had everything in common.
They sold property and possessions to give to those in need.

We see corporate behaviors leading to personal salvations. But it was what individuals were doing together, to and for each other—and not what the institution was doing to or for its members. "They" activities are at the heart of corporate macro-addition capacity and of living in common.

At the same time, we're called to "live deployed." We each have a mission field of influence and a specific gifting. We are to "live deployed" via that unique calling.

In his book, *Real-Time Connections: Linking Your Job With God's Global Work*, Northwood Church planter/pastor Bob Roberts Jr., shares the insights he gleaned when he realized that God has called the whole Church—not just vocational missionaries—to live deployed.

"Rather than encouraging people to use their vocations to serve the church, what if we made it the church's task to mobilize Christians to use their everyday vocations to serve people in need—both locally and globally?" Roberts writes. "What would happen if Christians used their jobs, skills and passions to directly answer Christ's call to minister to those in need? What if we started to feed the hungry, clothe the naked, minister to the oppressed, and shelter the homeless? Could this be God's plan for reaching the nations and fulfilling the Great Commission?"[1]

This seismic shift in thinking inverted Roberts' approach to evangelism: "Instead of focusing on building a church by bringing people into it," he writes, "we focused on being missionaries to our area, making disciples who would fill churches."[2]

Creating and Managing Tensions

This dual command to live in common and to simultaneously live deployed often creates a tension in our churches. We need people to use their gifts as part of our addition-capacity activities. Local churches need all kinds of volunteers—greeters, ushers, set-up and teardown crews, small group leaders, nursery workers, student ministry volunteers, hospitality teams, etc. Unfortunately, in our zeal to create addition-growth capacity and "feed the beast" through volunteers, we often miss or even mute this dimension of "living deployed" to "release the beast." The average church doesn't see equipping and mobilizing people to *go* and be missionaries in their communities as their role. Instead, volunteers are primarily recruited and mobilized to "run" the church.

Think about an aircraft carrier. What distinguishes the aircraft carrier from a cruise ship? Its mission is to send air power to places the carrier can't go. A carrier without planes would simply be a floating cruise ship. In a similar way, the mission of the church is to carry the fullness of Jesus into the world. A church without deployed missionaries is most likely an ever-enlarging cruise ship filled with cultural Christians.

Within this addition-growth culture, churches experience a real and challenging tension: people lead busy lives. Instead of seeing church as a family positioned at the center of life, church becomes just one of the many commitments throughout the week. Thus, we tend to put some form of "pick three" in place. How many times have you heard churches call their members to commit to three things: (1) attend Sunday services; (2) get into a small group; and (3) spend an hour volunteering at church (often during one of the worship services). Our addition-growth strategies take 100 percent of a member's allocated time, with no margin for equipping and mobilization beyond the walls of the church.

When this happens, we end up creating tension for people: choose between participating in a small group and serving as a volunteer. Notice how this tension is between priorities within the "living in common" (local church context) rather than the "living deployed" dimension. This is how accumulation growth cultures neuter the mobilization dimension—cutting multiplication potential off at the knees.

Some churches are even satisfied with allowing members to "pick one" (small groups or volunteering), thereby alleviating the tension altogether.

Small Groups ⟵ **Growth Strategies** ⟶ **Mobilizing Volunteers**

This is not the way Jesus intended the Church to function. God has designed each of us to live in common, doing whatever we need to do to support the church body, while simultaneously going into our unique corners of society. When people aren't using their unique calling and gifts to *go*, as leaders we negatively impact Jesus' mission for His Church. When we do find ways to lead our churches so that we're simultaneously living in common *and* living deployed, we mobilize biblical disciples to go and be Kingdom Multipliers!

Mobilization Motives

When it comes to mobilization, you can put churches into one of three categories, based on their underlying motives for mobilization. First, most churches focus on *mobilizing volunteers* to fill the service opportunities inside the church. Running Sunday services and ministry programming requires significant volunteer hours. These churches prioritize the first fruits of volunteers to running internal programming requirements.

Second, some churches focus on *mobilizing leaders* to help scale the addition (and sometimes multiplication) capacity of the church (see chapter 8 for more on capacity building). In most cases, leadership development systems and pipelines are the next natural progression of building addition capacity. Leadership development is an essential element for both addition and multiplication capacity. The only question is whether or not the primary motive for leadership development is building addition capacity or multiplication capacity.

Third, few churches focus on *mobilizing everyday missionaries* to carry the fullness of Jesus into every crack and cranny of society. Most churches don't focus on "living deployed" practices like helping people understand their unique personal calling; equipping them to be missionaries; and helping them claim a mission field in their unique corner of society. This third motivation requires a church to flip itself upside down. Instead of mobilizing volunteers to build capacity to attract, serve, and accumulate more people, this third category of churches sees developing and deploying everyday missionaries to their unique corners of society as its role. Level 5 multiplication requires this type of radical, counter- church culture commitment.

With 96 percent of churches never reproducing, we can safely conclude that the first category or motivation is the prevailing approach in church (mobilizing volunteers). While the growing numbers of churches with leadership development systems is encouraging, it's also safe to assume that most of these emerging approaches are strategies for building addition capacity rather than multiplication capacity.

A Balancing Act

The three core dimensions of multiplication—disciple making, capacity building and mobilization—require an intentional, disciplined balancing act to ensure we manage the tensions at each end to give us the genius of the *and*. We need to add disciples *and* multiply disciples; build addition capacity *and* build multiplication capacity; and we need to live in common *and* live deployed.

Each of the three elements has a natural addition and multiplication tension. Without our intervention, the natural tensions are:

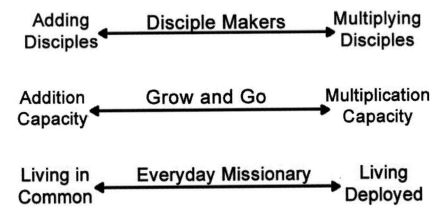

We balance these tensions by focusing on making disciple makers, creating cultures that simultaneously value growing and going, and making everyday missionaries. Notice there are three addition elements (the left side) and three corresponding multiplication elements (the right side). We get in trouble when we replace the multiplication elements with addition elements. This produces tensions such as:

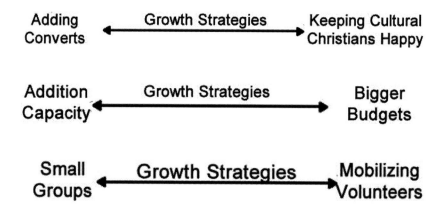

Notice that our focus on Level 3 growth strategies takes the place of focusing on making disciple makers, creating a sending culture, and making everyday missionaries. Our internal focus on Level 3 growth strategies takes our eyes and attention off multiplication. The result? Less than 4 percent of U.S. churches ever reproduce.

Some models are rooted in Level 3 addition and will naturally lead us away from multiplication. It's critical hat we define our priorities for addition AND multiplication, and then embrace models that can deliver our desired outcomes. In the next chapter, we'll look at the characteristics of models and five key shifts that will position and empower us to more naturally embrace and focus on the three dimensions of multiplication.

Putting It into Practice

• *How would you define and describe the difference between "living in common" and "living deployed"?*

• *How do these two dimensions create a natural tension for you and other church leaders?*

• *Do you see your church as an army of missionaries with the capacity to fill every crack and cranny of your community?*

• *If you started measuring your success by how well you deploy your members as everyday missionaries into your community, what would have to change about how your church functions?*

• *"From volunteer to missionary"—what excites you about this shift? What scares or intimidates you?*

• *In what ways do you integrate regular stories of community engagement and impact in your sermons, newsletters, printed materials, etc.?*

FREE Tools for Multipliers

Church Assessment on Capacity Building
I strongly encourage you to spend thirty minutes taking the FREE online church multiplication assessment available at www.becomingfive.org. The assessment measures your church's cultural capacity for multiplication. You'll receive immediate results, including a Multiplication Score (Level 1 through 5) and a Multiplication Pattern. This information is essential for finding your specific multiplication pathway.

Enter your assessment scores below:

My Multiplication
Capacity Score: Level 1   2   3   4   5

My Multiplication
Capacity Pattern: _____

Disciple Maker Assessment. This online resource is an effective tool for helping you change your scorecard to focus on the Church's core purpose of biblical disciple making. In twenty minutes, you'll receive results indicating your past, present and future effectiveness as a disciple maker.

HeroMaker Assessment. This online resource is an effective tool for helping you measure your personal leadership capacity and to what degree you're balancing addition and multiplication. In twenty minutes, you'll receive results indicating your past, present and future effectiveness as a Level 5 Multiplier.

Dream Big Workbook by Will Mancini. Chapter 2 includes an entire section to help you see how each of the three dimensions of multiplication work together for the core purpose of making, multiplying and mobilizing disciples. The workbook also includes questions and exercises to work through individually and as a team.

Chapter 10
Models

*Insanity: Continuing to do the same things
over and over again, but expecting different results.*
~author unknown

Why would we think that more of the same Level 3 thinking and behaviors that have firmly established our Level 3 scorecards will somehow start producing Level 5 multiplication results? As Multipliers, we could define insanity as "continuing to value the same addition/accumulation-focused thinking and behaviors, but expecting to see multiplication results!"

Without a new generation of Level 5 Multipliers who throw off the old wineskins and embrace new models, we're unlikely to see multiplication results. Speed of the leader … speed of the team! We need fresh expressions of church that will more naturally let us embrace and focus on what we've been talking about in the last two chapters—making disciple makers, building multiplication capacity, and mobilizing everyday missionaries.

When we began writing the Exponential anchor books, *Spark* and *Becoming a Level 5 Multiplying Church*, the lack of Level 5 benchmark churches limited our ability to quantitatively define Level 5 church characteristics. To steward the multiplication conversation and better define the five levels of multiplication, Exponential formed a working team of national leaders from various multiplication ministries and Level 4 and 5 churches. We meet several times throughout the year to focus on the characteristics of Level 5 churches. Over the last two years, the team has identified ten characteristics of the Level 5 church of the future (see our free eBook, *Dream Big, Plan Smart*, for a more detailed explanation of these ten characteristics). The characteristics include:

- Jesus is Lord
- Culture of Biblical Disciple Making
- New Measures of Success/Scorecards
- Empowering Systems
  - A bias to "yes"
  - A sending impulse
  - Easily accessible (everyone gets to play)
  - A minimal ecclesiology
  - Messy, insecure and risky
- Adaptive Systems, including Liberated Financial Systems
- Apostolic Atmosphere
- Level 5 Leadership (Level 5 HeroMaking Multipliers)
- Kingdom-centric/Geo-centric Focus
- Relational Affiliation to a Tribe, Family or Network of Churches
- Everyone a Missionary

Creating a culture of multiplication around the ten characteristics of Level 5 churches requires a shift in our paradigm. Embracing these characteristics and choosing a model that naturally brings these characteristics to life are primary roles of Level 5 Multipliers. The national team of leaders collaborating to identify these characteristics has also identified five key shifts in our paradigm that are essential to creating a culture of multiplication. Notice how these specific shifts align with what we've been talking about over the last nine chapters.

These shifts, as articulated by discipleship author and speaker Dave Rhodes, include:

1. A shift in the hero story for the primary leader...*from being the hero to becoming the mentor who creates heroes that become mentors.*

Becoming a Level 5 church starts with the pursuit of becoming a Level 5 leader. As we discussed n chapter 6, every true shift in a church or organization begins with a personal or heart change in the primary leader—a change in your personal

100

scorecard. Story after story tells us that leaders who want to see change organizationally but don't take the time to make the necessary personal shifts will rarely experience the results they desire. Marked by a sense of holy and humble tenacity, the Level 5 leader shifts from being simply the hero of the church and instead uses his/her power and influence in a mentoring role to help others become the heroes and the future mentors the church will need.

2. A shift in expectation for every believer...*from being consumers or converts to being disciples who make disciples who make disciples to the fourth generation.*

As you know by now, biblical disciple making is the core of healthy Kingdom multiplication. To shift from being a community of consumers coming each week to gain their spiritual fix, the Level 5 church trains their people in the character and competency of Jesus, empowering and equipping them to make disciples who make disciples to the fourth generation. This means that Level 5 leaders start asking future questions: How many fourth-generation disciples does our church have? Have we seen that number increase from last year to this year? Is what I'm doing now as a leader going to get us to the fourth generation?

3. A shift in opportunity for every disciple...*from being a volunteer in a church to becoming a missionary to a mission field waiting to be declared.*

This distinctive may be the most important of any of the shifts. Level 5 leaders take the priesthood of believers seriously. To become disciples who make disciples who make disciples, people must start thinking of themselves differently—as potential pastors or missionaries with a church waiting to be birthed among those with whom they live, work and play.

4. A shift in operation for the system...*from the bias of "no" to the bias of "yes."*

Becoming a Level 5 church means shifting the systems of the church, being open to redefining what a church is, and then leaders helping people learn to live with the sense of permission that's already inside of them. Uncovering this inherent permission allows us to step into everything God has called us to be and do.

When we shift the operation system, we redesign our systems to move from, "We can do it; you can help," to, "You can do it; we can help." We develop adaptive and empowering systems that change and shift quickly to move from high command and control at the center, to creating a culture at the edges that quickly and easily says "yes." By clearly defining our core mission (making disciples), we can decentralize, allowing our church to adapt and multiply into new contexts without spending unnecessary time on bureaucratic decision-making.

5. A shift in the scorecard...*from counting the number of people in any one church to the percentage of a population changed. From accumulation to transformation.*

Level 5 leaders measure success differently than other churches. Instead of just counting the number of people who come to the church, Level 5 leaders are more concerned with the growth of the Kingdom among their surrounding neighborhoods and networks. Functioning from a collaborative Kingdom mindset, this means creating change within a population distinctive that's bigger than what any one church could do on its own. This shift requires us to create networks or families of churches that work together to see the "win."

The Role of Level 5 Multipliers

Level 5 churches must be led by Level 5 leaders who are passionate about creating and maintaining a biblical culture of multiplication. So far, we've identified several integrated areas that shape a Level 5 Multiplier. Level 5 leaders should:

- Have the courage to surrender their egocentric scorecards and embrace a multiplication scorecard (chapter 6).

- Understand, own, and manage the three dimensions of healthy multiplication: disciple making, capacity building, and empowering systems for mobilization (chapters 8 and 9).

- Understand, own, and manage the ten characteristics of a Level 5 culture (described above and in *Dream Big, Plan Smart*).

- Understand, own, and manage the five paradigm shifts required for creating Level 5 culture (discussed above and in *Dream Big, Plan Smart*).

- Be diligent at considering fresh expressions and models for the future that will more naturally promote a culture of multiplication (the rest of this chapter highlights the emerging micro-church era).

The Emerging Micro-Church Era

As we look at future models that organically enable and empower multiplication, the emerging micro-church era should be on our radar. The following exploration derives from a white paper Exponential released in April 2017. As you read it, think about the micro-church expressions you've already seen and how you might respond as a leader focused on multiplication, not addition.

It doesn't take a rocket scientist to see what's coming next in the Western church. It has taken thirty years to move from less than one hundred megachurches to over 7,000 and ten years to move from less than one hundred multisite churches to more than 2,000. Although God's fingerprints are all over the numerical growth of these movements, neither the MEGA nor the MULTI appear to be His destination. Instead, they appear to be the means to an end.

Increasingly, we can connect the dots and see that they are part of a bigger, ongoing journey to an even better place—from MEGA to MULTI to MICRO.

What if God has uniquely positioned the prevailing MEGA/MULTI church as the distribution system for the MICRO? Contrary to what many would like to see, the deconstruction or bashing of the prevailing MEGA/MULTI is like shooting the goose laying the golden eggs. Instead, what if we were to celebrate and catalyze its incredible capacity to propel the MICRO forward in a more viral way than we've ever seen in North America.

As Exponential continues to look for new wineskins necessary for Level 5 multiplication in the United States, we see a potential awakening for the Church. This new emerging era of micro-focused churches is now positioned to produce a much-needed fresh wind and reformation in the Church. *Or*, conversely, it could represent a major distraction and barrier to multiplication.

Although there is no universally accepted definition of "micro-focused," the following description will help you work through this chapter: *"Micro-focused" represents expressions of church that aim toward carrying the fullness of Jesus into every crack and cranny of society instead of seeking to draw people to one (or a limited number) of centralized gathering locations.*

Think of micro-focused as fully functioning, decentralized outposts of a church, without the traditional staff, facilities, programming, complexity, and cost. Micro-focused expressions are often the benefactor of support systems from a larger governing organization, but with increased autonomy compared with a multisite campus. Micro-focused expressions may be described as "microsites," "micro-churches," "mini-churches," etc.

Evolutionary Versus Revolutionary Change

As churches struggle with the cost, staffing, and organizational complexities needed to reproduce campuses and look for easier options, these emerging "micro-focused" expressions appear to be a viable extension of the prevailing MEGA/MULTI models due to their flexibility, adaptability, and scalability. The home base provides the resources and content while the micro-focused structures provide the distribution channels.

Ironically, most of the new micro pathways are emerging out of the inevitable discontent that larger, influential churches are experiencing in their pursuit of addition growth. As this next season unfolds, we should pay close attention to whether more dramatic and *revolutionary* change occurs and shifts our basic paradigms toward Level 5 multiplication. *Or* whether these new expressions are rooted in *evolutionary* and incremental change to optimize addition-growth strategies, thus stifling multiplication. This conversation leads to an important and yet-to-be-answered question: *Is it even possible to create scalable reproduction within our addition-addicted culture?* With evolutionary change, these new expressions will simply decentralize and further optimize the, "we can do it, you can help" bias of accumulation-focused churches.

Revolutionary change, however, will require a shift in:

- How we measure success in biblical disciple making;
- How we simultaneously build addition AND multiplication capacity;
- How we mobilize the priesthood of all believers within the context of each person's unique calling.

Revolutionary change will be less about fueling the gathering capacity of the local church, and more about releasing and mobilizing the sending capacity of the church into every crack and cranny of society. This requires a shift in the role of the church to one characterized by "you can do it, we can help." Unfortunately, if the past is predictive of the future, most of these emerging expressions will not fuel true biblical multiplication via revolutionary change.

Currently, many of the churches that fill the spots on the largest, fastest-growing, and most innovative churches lists are already shaping the conversation for this next micro-focused season. Some of these churches will likely pioneer important and revolutionary pathways into the future. Most, however, will perpetuate biases that actually inhibit multiplication.

If micro-focused churches are solid models for multiplication, we need to consider some important questions:

How do we thoughtfully and intentionally engage in a way that honors God, propels the mission of the Church, and produces the fruit of biblical multiplication?

How do we ensure the fruit of our labor yields sustainable Level 5 multiplying churches rather than simply optimizing new strategies for Level 3 constrained expressions of church?

How do we position ourselves and our churches to be the best possible stewards of this emerging era of "micro-focused" churches?

There is much to be excited about in this emerging era of the micro-focused church. The micro has the potential to mobilize everyday missionaries into every crack and cranny of society. However, it's easy to become infatuated with the next emerging growth opportunity and completely miss the multiplication potential. We must discern if a core DNA that successfully attracts, catches, and accumulates large crowds is the same DNA that can reproduce, release, and send Christ followers into every corner of society.

This next season of "micro-focused" churches has the potential to be implemented as either simple evolutionary change that optimizes new growth strategies, or as radical revolutionary change that fuels biblical multiplication as our Founder intended it to be. Exponential is jumping in to help shape the future conversation toward multiplication.

How Will Your Church Respond? Ten Questions to Consider

1. *Is micro-church the right next step for us?* Focus on answering the other nine questions below, and you'll probably have your answer to this one.

Multipliers learn from the multisite movement of the past fifteen years. According to Leadership Network, the number of multisite churches in the United States has swelled from less than one hundred to more than 8,000 in that period of time. This movement has accelerated the impact of thousands of churches and moved some from Level 3 addition to Level 4 reproduction. That's great news!

However, the move to multisite has also inhibited the multiplication behaviors of many churches, including a large number that should have never pursued multisite. It has been easy for churches to become captivated by the promise and trend of multisite without first being diligent to understand the potential opportunity, costs, risks, and rewards of their decision.

Micro-focused church is an emerging trend that will gain popularity and momentum. Like multisite, it will be right for some churches and wrong for others. Be proactive in engaging (or dismissing) it for the right reasons and motives.

2. *What is our motive for considering micro-church?* This question might be the single most important one you ask as a Multiplier. Our motives tend to define our priorities, behaviors and ultimately, our results. At the highest level, are you driven by addition, reproduction, or multiplication? Are you satisfied being the very best Level 3 church you can be, growing as large as you can and reaching as many people as possible? Or are you seeking to become a Multiplier and move to Levels 4 and 5 that require a new scorecard and operating system?

At the more detailed level of perspective, you have numerous possible answers to your motivation questions. Keep asking "why" until you get to your one root or core reason for going micro. Don't stop with easy answers like, "to reach more people." Instead, turn it around and ask, "Why is micro-church the best possible way for us to reach more people?" In the same way, continue turning each answer into another "why" question until you arrive at your core motive.

With your team, press into the difference between addition, reproduction and multiplication in your context. Spend the necessary time to discern what your core motives are about. Are they focused on addition (Level 3 behaviors), reproduction (Level 4 behaviors), or multiplication (Level 5 behaviors)?

Evolutionary change is safe and easy, but it defaults to Level 3 behaviors. At Level 3, our current behaviors just extend into new locations. Results are often additive as you seek to conquer the next growth barrier. Level 3 churches continue to be centrally controlled and governed, and rooted in a bias toward, "we can do it, you can help." The Level 3 scorecard ultimately and honestly boils down to accumulation.

Now look at Level 5 multiplication behaviors. They are risky and require more radical, revolutionary change. They also require that you change the status quo and your operating system. It's not about simply extending what you already have into a new context. With a Level 5 motive, you're driven by things like improving the quality of your disciple making; shifting your scorecard to measure success by what you send and release rather than what you accumulate; building multiplication capacity to accelerate impact far beyond your local context; and releasing the priesthood of all believers within the context of each person's unique calling and mission field. It's about building a legacy through the impact of the future versus the accumulation of the present. Level 5 motives result in decentralized control that shifts your bias to, "you can do it, how can we help?"

Are you motivated by Level 3 addition, Level 4 reproduction, or Level 5 multiplication? It's a tough question, but an important shaping factor in how you'll implement micro-church. Be honest about your motives. If being the best Level 3 church is your vision, do it with excellence. If the Holy Spirit is convicting you to develop a Level 4 or 5 motive, use the micro expression to help guide your path. It might be difficult to fully discern your answer without first considering the reality of how you're living out your core values.

3. *How do our core values impact our decision about micro-church?* While your core values don't necessarily shape *what* you do, they do have more impact than anything else in shaping *how* you do whatever you do. Your core values aren't defined by what you *say* is important to you. Rather, your actions and behaviors define your values. Less than 4 percent of U.S. churches ever demonstrate the behavior of reproducing or multiplying. What does that say about the core value of reproduction or multiplication in the U.S. Church today?

Which value have your past behaviors been most closely aligned to? Addition, reproduction, or multiplication? Which value is most likely to shape your implementation of micro-churches? Before making a decision about micro-church, does any work need to be done to adjust (or affirm) your core values? Which core values are impacting your motives for pursuing micro-churches?

4. *What does micro-church look like in our context?* To answer that question, you must first understand the context for this new era of micro-church. It grows out of the natural evolution and progression from megachurch to multisite to now, micro. Churches will naturally extrapolate the strengths and benefits of the MEGA and MULTI models and adapt them into the MICRO. Consequently, for most churches the default approach will be extending what's already being done into new locations.

Most churches will likely be attracted to the potential for replicating their training content/Sunday programming into new, extended, lower-cost venues that have the potential to reach more people (the love language of Level 3 addition-focused churches). The most natural expression equates to the convergence of small groups, technology, high-quality training materials, and decentralized delivery systems—all within our current grasp.

For example, a typical leadership conversation might go like this: "We already put so much overhead effort into producing training materials and Sunday services. Why don't we establish more gathering locations for delivering our content? What if we decentralized smaller group gatherings that don't require special facilities or staff? Full-service locations are so expensive, slow to start, and require so much overhead and oversight. What if we trained key leaders to facilitate micro-churches? We could extend the impact of what we're already doing without significantly adding costs. Oh, but wait. What about tithes and offerings? Will we hurt our financial giving by allowing people to do church without coming to the big box?"

Enter technology and the embracement of online giving. Technology is now at a point where most key drivers of a centralized large group church gathering can be efficiently and effectively decentralized with volunteer leadership.

Extension is easier, safer, cheaper, and more consistent in its implementation. The MEGA and MULTI expressions scale efficiently because they're franchise models. Although they may look differently on the surface, 90-plus percent of MEGA/MULTI models are the same under the hood. They scale more easily because they grow out of proven, reproducible systems. The default context for micro-church will also be a franchise model. The benefits include scalability at a lower cost; accelerated attendance numbers; quality control through a centralized system; and consistency of message.

So it's important to ask and honestly answer: *Will we use a franchise model to reproduce and scale micro-churches with consistency, or will we take a more boutique approach to start a wide range of custom contexts?*

The former is much simpler. It's evolutionary—an extension of what already is. The franchise model lives at the core of Level 3 growth strategies. The latter requires a new operating system to support. It's far more radical and revolutionary. But that's what characterizes Level 5 multiplying churches and is a critical reason why we have so few of them. Consequently, few churches will choose custom contexts as their default approach to micro-churches.

Still, the fact that we even have such a significant and transformative option available to us is profoundly significant. Just having the boutique option means that some percentage of churches will take it. Connect the dots, and we wind up with an increasing number of Level 5 churches. That's exciting! It will change the look of eternity.

The Underground Network based in Tampa Bay, Florida, is seeing the impact of approaching micro-church in custom contexts. The Underground is a fellowship of 150-plus micro-churches with the larger church expression serving the smaller. The church mobilizes, resources and empowers these groups, as individuals—not the leaders—start and lead these fresh expressions of faith that reach into every corner of society. Groups reach out to their neighbors (home-based churches), certain populations (mission-based churches), university students (campus-based churches) and to those that labor globally to share the gospel (global movements). Leader Brian Sanders is convicted that people (not buildings, budgets or leaders) make up the church.

Another question you need to ask, then, is, *Are we biased to creating more gathering opportunities, or to creating more deployment opportunities?*

Creating more gathering opportunities is evolutionary and safe. It's Level 3 thinking. Creating more custom deployment opportunities is far more chaotic and uncertain. It represents Level 5 thinking. The difference is subtle but profound if we're to unlock the huge pent-up capacity of the priesthood of all believers. Essentially, are we building more aircraft carriers, or are we creating more missions for planes to fly? Will your micro-church context be about adding gatherings to deliver your content and message, or about outposts for delivering the love of Jesus to every crack and cranny of society?

The local church is the best mobilizer of volunteers on the planet … for *our* purposes. We know how to fill the volunteer roles that fuel the Level 3 growth engine. Micro-church now provides us with the context to mobilize the priesthood of all believers in ways the U.S. Church has never seen. Micro-church provides a unique opportunity for equipping, deploying, and sending believers in the context of their unique personal calling and mission field. Level 5 multiplication is as much about mobilization as it is about building larger gatherings. It requires that we shift our bias to, "you can do it, how can we help?" Instead of a bias to "no" because an idea doesn't fit our agenda, we must look for and celebrate the "yes" when it represents mobilizing and sending a believer on mission to a new context, equipped with their unique personal calling. Unfortunately, the prevailing systems in church are not designed to support this approach.

Will you start a franchise or a boutique ministry? Will you focus primarily on creating new gathering opportunities or on mobilizing an army of missionaries into every cranny of society?

5. *What does "wildly successful" look like in our context? Will our default way of implementing micro-churches produce the transformative impact we're searching for?* At this point, you may not yet have a clear picture of what micro-churches would look like in your context. Spend some time thinking through what outcomes you're hoping to achieve. What scorecard would you use for defining success, and what specific metrics will you measure to ensure the outcomes are worth the effort? Dream a bit and paint a picture of what a wildly successful micro-church would look like? What results and impact would they produce?

Lead your team to think through specific questions related to these four factors:

- In what ways will you seek to leverage micro-churches for improving your church health in each area?
- In what ways will you approach disciple making differently in micro-churches than in your other expressions of church?
- How will you leverage micro-churches to increase your capacity for starting new autonomous churches that reach people beyond your local context?
- How will your approach to deploying people within the context of their unique calling differ in micro-churches?

Try this simple exercise. Suppose your church starts its first micro-church in the next few weeks. It's wildly successful. Some church members say it's the most successful thing you've ever done as a church. You're so energized you want to start one hundred of them in the next year. Now, make a list of the specific outcomes that would create this level of excitement, enthusiasm, and urgency.

Will the default evolutionary path produce the success you're looking for, or is more revolutionary change needed in your context? Why or why not?

6. *What strengths are we building on, and how might these strengths create limitations to true multiplication if we're not careful?* It's natural to build new things on the solid foundation of what's already proven and working. There's good stewardship in this principle. This approach is safer in the franchise approach compared with the custom or boutique approach. In the franchise approach, you're seeking to replicate the best of your proven things into new contexts. However, in the boutique or custom approach, the "proven" may actually hinder your ability to reach into new contexts or people groups. Consider this example:

113

A volunteer leader in a large local church is passionate about his community and is relationally connected to many of his neighbors, but has been unable to convince his friends and neighbors to drive the forty-five minutes to the nearest campus location. He lives with a tension of wanting to spend more time serving and ministering to his neighbors but is constrained by the hour-and-a-half round trip to church (and his volunteer time there). He's thrilled when his church decides to start micro-sites with the franchise model—small groups meeting in remote locations using video for their teaching. Because preaching and worship are the top strengths for attracting the largely Boomer membership to the main location, the church's franchise approach requires that all of its microsites use the same worship and preaching on video from the main location.

However, this passionate volunteer starts a micro-site in a community of young Millennial couples who are newly married and are struggling with the tensions of balancing marriage, work, and young children. They continually turn to the volunteer leader for advice and counsel. Recognizing that more than half the couples coming to this micro-site need a solid biblical series on marriage, the volunteer leader requests permission to deviate from the norm and do a special series on marriage. He even recommends a specific six-week video series by Francis and Lisa Chan. Most of the people in the group have heard of Francis Chan and are excited to invite their friends. Unfortunately, the large church denies the request because it's inconsistent with the church's franchise model.

Many churches considering micro-focused church are intrigued by this idea of replicating their teaching and worship into new locations at a lower cost. Pause and consider the difference between what it looks like to replicate teaching and worship in a franchise versus a boutique (custom) context. Think about it like this. The franchise model is like a radio station. The listener has no option other than the songs the station plays. The fact that she wants or needs specific music doesn't matter. Her option is to listen to what the station programs. The boutique or custom model is like an iTunes playlist. The user decides what content to play.

In the franchise church model, the church provides content to volunteer leaders. In the boutique model, the church helps equip the volunteer leader to select and customize the best possible content to suit the needs of the group, even if it comes from leaders of other churches/ministries. The difference may sound minor, but it's the difference in Level 3 accumulation and Level 5 multiplication thinking.

Most churches considering micro-church can handle the support systems the franchise model requires; much of that infrastructure is already in place for their full-campus sites. The boutique/custom approach requires a new way of thinking and organizing. Additionally, a few "egos" will need to get out of the way.

Will you offer a radio station or a custom playlist?

As you think about your potential context for micro-focused church, what strengths are important to build on? What strengths and features from the "come and see" context are worthy enough to carry to the frontlines where micro-church happens? Which elements are "core," and which are "supporting"? What pitfalls might you experience in seeking to extend these strengths into the micro-church context?

7. *What barriers are we likely to face?* Barriers and obstacles are a natural reality in life. Regardless of our church model or approach, we will hit barriers. Micro-focused churches will solve some obstacles that the MEGA/MULTI church faces, but they will also introduce new, and possibly unexpected, barriers.

In implementing micro-churches, you'll have the obvious implementation and change management challenges. New and different things always cause some resistance. You're probably already familiar with and used to dealing with these types of barriers. Let's focus, instead, on the potential barriers unique to scaling micro-churches.

Although reproducing multiple campuses is a form of scaling, the micro-focus may lead you to reproducing hundreds (or even thousands) of sites. This kind of reproduction will present new challenges you don't currently face. As you begin to think about potential barriers, look back at your definition of "wildly successful." What type of support structure will you need for micro-church? Is your support structure capable of scaling to one hundred-plus sites? One campus of 1,000 people led by full-time staff will take fifty micro-sites of twenty people to get to the same 1,000. These fifty sites will likely be led by volunteers who need support. Further, the boutique versus franchise model will be even more chaotic.

In addition to scaling barriers, other issues will need to be addressed, including theology, governance, and leadership. In the franchise approach, the solution may be similar to how you handle small groups. However, in the boutique or custom approach, you're pioneering new territory. So don't be caught off guard.

8. *Does the simplicity/complexity of our strategy inherently catalyze or hinder multiplication?*
Consider the growth of the megachurch, the reproducing of sites or campuses, and the starting of autonomous new churches. What do they all have in common? Complexity, large budgets, and reliance on paid, professional staff. We create systems and machines that are difficult for the average Christ follower to start and lead. Consequently, we fuel our, "we can do it, you can help" bias, as our critical resource becomes the volunteer hours required to help run the machine and support operations. Historically, the ability to hire paid staff and mobilize enough volunteers limits the Level 3
addition-focused church.

In implementing micro-churches, will you intentionally take advantage of the potential for simplifying things, or will your approach add to your complexity? What will it look like to implement an approach that's not constrained by paid staff, budgets, and facilities? Will the average Christ follower be able to jump in and start a micro-church without significant obstacles and challenges? To what degree will you allow decision-making and control to be decentralized to the front lines?

As you consider micro-focused churches, be intentional about keeping things simple. Let "intentional simplicity" be a guiding value. Implement approaches that liberate your members and give them permission, encouragement, and accountability to mobilize within the context of their unique personal calling and mission field. Above all, be relentless on avoiding any complexity that hinders a multiplication impulse.

9. *What is our minimum ecclesiology for the structure and governance of church? Will that hinder true multiplication?* Every church considering micro-focused expressions will need to deal with the issue of theology, structure, leadership and governance (or decision making). For many networks and denominations, these are hot topics and may be the greatest limiting factors to multiplication. Most of the issues center around how churches will exercise central control and the level of autonomy decentralized to the front lines. Wrestling with these issues early is essential. Otherwise, your design will be significantly constrained and naturally limited to Level 3 biases.

The key questions to work through include:

What is our minimum definition of church? If three people gather weekly in a home as part of a microsite, is that church? Will we have minimum expectations of what they must do to count this as "church," eliminating the need to attend the large group gathering at a main location? What about teaching, communion, prayer, worship, etc.?

For example, if a store manager wants to start a micro-church in her workplace and declares herself the pastor of the shopping mall, what is the minimum "function" that needs to happen to officially call this "church"? Or if a coach wants to declare his community baseball team his micro-church, will you allow that? If so, what are the functional requirements to make this group a "real church?"

For further discussion, create your own scenarios that involve mobilizing and deploying your members into the corners of society where they already are. Proactively address the issues of what "church" means in this context.

What structural issues will shape our strategy? The three big factors to consider are the role of paid staff in supporting/overseeing the micro-churches; the organizational structure for micro-churches, including support services and how they fit within the overall church; and the budget/flow of money. For example, will tithes and offerings stay with the micro-church for use at their discretion, or will funds flow back to the central church for use in the general budget? Be proactive in identifying and defining clear expectations.

What governance and decision-making controls will apply to our micro-churches? This may be the elephant in the room that distinguishes Level 3 and 4 expressions from Level 5 multiplication. Franchise organizations scale, in part, because of the strong and clear controls they have in place. When I visit a Chick-fil-A location, I know I'll receive consistent service and food. It's the consistent experience that keeps me coming back. And it's the clear central controls that are pushed to the front lines that help guarantee consistency in any location.

Despite the benefits, however, central control also stifles innovation and multiplication on the fringes. For this reason, modern management pioneer Peter Drucker was adamant that organizations should position new R&D projects outside their normal control boundaries as separate autonomy for decision-making.

You must wrestle with the decision of how much autonomy to give micro-churches. In general, the franchise model can tolerate more controls. The boutique or custom approach that takes different shapes in different contexts will require more autonomy.

Finally, many of the leading multisite churches have scaled to between five and ten locations. Looking ahead, many of these churches are coming to grips with the Asymptote Principle (described in chapter 5), which essentially means that instead of getting easier with each additional location, scaling gets more difficult and more complex. Many of these churches reorganize every few years (or continually) to deal with the complexity. Don't miss the fact that the primary factor in scaling complexity and dynamics is governance. Central control and authority will always slow things down. Initially, the first fifty micro-sites may be easier than five full-service campuses. But eventually, centralized governance will limit the scaling of micro-sites the same way it limits full campuses.

To the greatest extent possible, decentralize and push governance to the fringes!

10. *Where are we on the innovation curve, and how does this affect our decision?*
When Leadership Network convened some pioneering churches in 2001, multisite was an "innovation." Many of these churches created the maps for the rest of the church world. Experts suggest that at the time, only a handful of multisite churches existed in the United States. Today, less than twenty years later, Leadership Network reports more than 8,000 multisite churches.

This increase represents what communications professor Everett Rodgers popularized as the *diffusion of innovation* theory. Rodgers sought to explain how some ideas turn into innovations that spread to the masses. He identified five categories of innovation "adopters," including innovators (the pioneers that create the maps for everyone else, representing 2.5 percent of a population); early adopters (the people who first embrace the innovation before it's even fully proven, representing 13.5 percent); the early majority

(34 percent); the late majority (also 34 percent), and the laggards (16 percent).

Let's assume micro-focused churches are an innovation waiting to happen. Currently, we're in the early stages where the innovators (2.5 percent) will begin experimenting and creating the maps for the future. Where should your church be on the innovation curve? Don't jump too quickly. Where you *want* to be might not be where you *should* be!

Consider three questions:

- *Where do my heart and head say we'd like to be on the curve?* Your heart may be telling you one thing, but is it the right thing? Does your heart align with your head?

- *Where have we historically been on the curve with past innovations?* The past is our best predictor of the future. Do you have a pattern and history of being innovators, early adopters, early majority, late majority, or laggards? You may not know it, but a pattern is likely embedded into your DNA and culture, and that's hard to change.

- *Given the reality of our history and context, where is it prudent for us to be?* Should you wait for some roadmaps and stability to minimize risk? Or should you jump in early?[1]

As you approach these ten questions and work through your church's response, keep in mind both the potential opportunity for multiplication, as well as the potential distraction. Stewarded with multiplication as the goal, we have the potential to make quantum leaps toward seeing the less than 4 percent of churches in the United States increase to a Kingdom-advancing tipping point of 10 percent.

The emerging micro-church era offers real hope for carrying out Jesus' specific vision for His Church. In the next chapter, we're looking at that vision and how it changes you and your church as you become a Multiplier who leads beyond addition.

Putting It into Practice

• *"Jesus is Lord" is the first of the ten characteristics of Level 5 churches. What does this truth mean to you and your team? For this truth to play out in its fullest measure, what characteristics should a church hold up and value?*

• *What would it look like for a community of biblical disciple making to be wildly successful in a church?*

• *All churches want "everyone to play and be involved." What is the difference between Level 5 churches and other churches in how they seek to help people "play?"*

• *In chapter 3 of Dream Big, Plan Smart, we offer a survey to help you evaluate each of the ten characteristics of Level 5 churches and the difficulty involved in implementing each characteristic in your context. Take some time to work through that survey with your team.*

• *Reread questions 2-10 for considering micro-church and then answer question 1:Is micro-church the right next step for us? Why or why not?*

exponential.org

Chapter 11
Multiplication Vision

"Now glory be to God, who by his mighty power at work within us is able to do far more than we would ever dare to ask or even dream of—infinitely beyond our highest prayers, desires, thoughts, or hopes" (Eph. 3:20, TLB).

I love what Paul says here in his letter to the church at Ephesus. God has big dreams for us—"infinitely beyond" anything we can fathom. What does that look like for you and your church?

In this chapter, we're building on the solid foundations for a new scorecard that we talked about in chapters 8 and 9. We're discussing the vital need to transform our current addition-focused vision into a vision rooted in multiplication and then to identify the pathway that gets us to our desired destination.

Like the picture on a puzzle box, your vision communicates a clear and compelling image of the future. Your multiplication pathway gives you the map for getting there. Together, they move forward your new multiplication-focused scorecard and give you tools for bringing everyone else along on the journey.

That said, here's the critical question: *How strongly is your vision rooted in making disciples who make disciples that plant churches that plant churches?*

A vision rooted in multiplication conveys a strong commitment to sending and releasing disciples to plant churches that plant churches. When our vision is greater than growing and expanding our own kingdom (your church, your network, your denomination, etc.), the fruit of disciple making produces churches that plant churches—ultimately growing and expanding God's Kingdom.

The Paradox of Vision

For church leaders, vision provides a bit of a paradox. On one hand, we know through Scripture that God will hold us accountable for being good stewards of the resources He entrusts to our care. We all want to face Jesus some day and hear Him say, "Well done, good and faithful servant." Like the servants in the parable of the talents, we must act to risk and extend the resources the Master gives us. Vision stretches us to be fruitful.

On the other hand, we know that God cares more about our faithfulness and surrender to Him and His plans than our man-made visions and strategies.

Consider the pursuits of Noah, Abraham, Peter, Paul, Nehemiah and Ruth. Were their visions clear and world-changing? Not at all. These leaders we look to didn't know what they were doing. Noah couldn't comprehend God's bigger picture. Abraham said "yes" and didn't even know where he was going. Peter and Paul had no human idea how God would use them in the greatest movement in history. Nehemiah simply wanted to rebuild some walls and had no idea of God's bigger vision to rescue His people. And Ruth, she died without knowing the real legacy she'd leave in Jesus' lineage.

The heroes of the faith were known more for their faithfulness to cooperate with and surrender to God than they were their vision or strategy. When Jesus shared the last supper with His disciples and prayed for them, He could have laid out the master plan and grand vision for a world movement. Instead, He prayed for their faithfulness and after His resurrection, gave them His Great Commission (Matt. 28:19) and the Holy Spirit.

We get in trouble not for our lack of vision, but for our lack of obedience to "go" rather than "stay," and "accumulate" rather than "send"—making cultural Christians instead of biblical disciples. When our vision is more about living *our* dreams than God's dreams and building *our* strategies rather than cooperating in His plans, our good intentions for multiplication will always fail.

Your key question is not, "Where do *I* want to go?" or "Who do *I* want my church to become?" but rather, "Where does *God* want our church to go?" and, "Who does *He* want us to become?" In his classic study, *Experiencing God,* author Henry Blackaby perfectly summarizes the approach we need to take in developing vision in this familiar statement: "Watch to see where God is working and join Him."[1] Perhaps a lesser-known Blackaby insight comes from his book, *Spiritual Leadership: Moving People on to God's Agenda.* Obedience, he says, is key.

"If Christians around the world were to suddenly renounce their personal agendas, their life goals and their aspirations, and begin responding in radical obedience to everything God showed them, the world would be turned upside down," Blackaby writes. "How do we know? Because that's what first-century Christians did, and the world is still talking about it."[2]

We need to discover God's dream and vision, and then build our dreams around His. Too many times, we do the reverse. Yes, you need a unique vision for where God wants to take you and your church. You also need a pathway for getting there. But God must be the source of both.

Jesus' Multiplication Vision

The dream God gives each of us exists as part of a bigger dream rooted in Scripture. Right before His ascension into Heaven, Jesus shared His dream for His Church—His vision for multiplication:

"You will receive power when the Holy Spirit comes up on you; and you will be my witnesses in Jerusalem, and in all Judea and Samaria, and to the ends of the earth" (Acts 1:8).

The vision that Jesus gave His present and future followers focused on a movement. He had a powerful vision of God's Kingdom coming on earth as it is in heaven. Through the Holy Spirit, we have the power to venture beyond our home base and ultimately take His Good News to every tribe and every nation so that one day, "at the name of Jesus every knee should bow ... and every tongue confess that Jesus Christ is Lord" (Phil. 2:10-11).

Jesus knew that gargantuan dream would not be accomplished with one or even 1 million churches. He is asking us as Christ followers and leaders of His church to join with Him to accomplish His mission and grow His Kingdom. In the process, He grows and matures us. If you don't already know it, having a God-sized vision is a true life-changer.

Allowing your heart and mind to pursue a vision that's bigger than you will change you in significant ways. When you begin to get a clear vision for multiplication both as a leader and for our church, you start to see how God prepares and shapes you for that vision.

A Vision for Multiplication Changes Your Questions

When it comes to vision, one question will lead to another. The size of your vision will often determine the types of questions you ask. Easily manageable smaller vision requires one set of questions while God-sized vision will lead you to ask an entirely different set of questions. Since co-founding Exponential and starting NewThing Network, Dave Ferguson's questions have changed with the size of his dreams.

"Ten years ago, our dream was to start a network of new churches, so I had to ask, *How can I attract, train and deploy church planters?* Now our dream is to see a movement of reproducing churches, so I'm asking, *How can I create systems that reproduce networks and attract, train and deploy apostolic leaders?"*

As you start to ask the challenging questions that will help lead you toward your multiplication vision and move your new scorecard forward, your questions for how you measure success will begin to change. While we may still ask, "How many people worshipped with us this weekend," a multiplication vision requires us to think toward the future:

- How many churches will we plant this year and over the next five years?
- Will we budget significantly for church multiplication (an actual line item)?
- How many new churches outside our own church will we support?
- Will we release and send out leaders to multiply churches—even the most valuable ones?
- How many people will we encourage to leave and start a new church?
- If we pursue multiplication and our weekend attendance goes down as a result, will we see ourselves as successful?

Your vision guides both your personal scorecard and scorecard for your church. The greater your multiplication vision, the more profound the questions you will ask and the more your scorecards will change.

A Vision for Multiplication Changes Your Prayers

A vision for multiplication that's too big for you and your church to accomplish through your own efforts and giftings will drive you to your knees. It keeps you looking to God and depending on Him.

For West Ridge Church Planter/Pastor Brian Bloye, prayer was a catalyst for becoming a Multiplier. Bloye has led West Ridge's transformation from a congregation focused on size and growth into a community bent on Kingdom multiplication.

"My initial vision when I planted West Ridge was to become the biggest church we could be and to reach as many people as we could. But as we grew, God began to work in me," Bloye explains. "I realized that God has not called His Church to my vision. He has something much bigger in mind. As I laid out this new multiplication vision, I knew that God was going to have to do a work in our staff, and in the leadership of our church. And then He was going to have to do a work in our church. Even though I knew it would be a hard work, I knew that if I was praying about multiplication, if I was praying about reproduction, if I was praying about sending, then I was praying in line with God's will. If you pray in line with God's will, you will begin to pray powerful prayers."

As Exponential has directed its focus, energy and resources to Kingdom multiplication, Dave Ferguson's prayers have changed. Each day in his journal, he writes "4% > 10%."

"Every day I pray, 'God, use Exponential to see the number of multiplying churches in the U.S. go from 4 percent to 10 percent'" he says, "and then, 'God, use NewThing to create a global movement of 10,000 multiplying churches.'"

A Vision for Multiplication Changes the People Around You

Vision is contagious. When we get a vision for multiplication and begin to share it, we start a chain reaction. Have you ever seen someone's soul awaken as he/she begins to wonder about the role he/she could play in advancing the Kingdom?

Think about whose Kingdom vision has influenced you and made you say, "I want to lead a church that follows the biblical call to multiply disciples." In the same way, your multiplication vision could actually be the match that starts a wildfire! Sharing a clear vision for multiplication will slowly begin to change the people in your path in several ways:

People start to take ownership of the vision. Following a multiplying leader removes much of the mystery about how to pursue a vision. Think for a moment about how the process of visionary leadership is multiplied and transferred as the lead visionary mentors key team players.

Will Mancini has served as a vision architect for hundreds of churches. We partnered with him to help us do what he does best (Will worked with us on *Dream Big, Plan Smart* and wrote our *Dream Big Workbook*). For more than a decade, he has come alongside teams to help them bring clarity to their vision. He can look back and see how his mentors' God-sized dreams have led him to where he is today.

"I remember serving on Bruce Wesley's leadership team at Clear Creek Community Church in Houston," Mancini recalls. "I learned a ton about decision-making, communication, integrity and self-discipline. Most importantly, I learned from Bruce's mastery of calling others to commitment. Without his model in my life, I never could have imagined transitioning to a coaching ministry."

Watching a leader achieve his/her dreams removes fear and insecurity for everyone else that might dare to dream. We all know church leaders that relegate visionary leadership to a select few. Scripture tells us that daring to imagine big things is the opportunity of every believer. *People begin to see themselves as visionaries, and recognize that everyone is part of the vision, and that everyone has a unique calling.*

Unfortunately, many church leaders don't empower lay leaders to play this kind of role. Instead, they are the "ball hogs" of the Kingdom, never allowing the fruit of Ephesians 4 to grow and mature. Paul tells us that God gives gifted men and woman to the Church to *equip* the saints for the work of ministry—not to *excuse* the saints from the work of ministry.

When you start to prioritize Kingdom growth over growing your own kingdom, that vision will change others—from the high capacity donor to the risk-taking lay leader, to the high school freshman in your student ministry. The key question for Multipliers is, "How are you preparing for and expecting the chain reaction of visionary leadership to take place and grow?"

A Vision for Multiplication Changes You

Multipliers who are pursuing Level 5 multiplication can easily look back to see how vision has changed them personally.

Currently, Dave Ferguson dreams of seeing his Chicago-based church move from Level 4 to Level 5 multiplication. That dream, he says, has transformed him: "Other than becoming a Christ-follower, making the decision to become a multiplying church and pursuing a multiplication vision has been the biggest change in my life as a church leader."

Below, Ferguson identifies the various ways his dream has changed him and other multiplying leaders:

A multiplication vision deepens your relationship with God. Think about how the vision that God gave Moses began to change not only him, but also his relationship with the God who called him out of the desert and into new life. At the crossroads of each and every challenge, Moses' respect for God and His Word grew. His trust in God's promises for a future land strengthened him in adversity. Throughout Exodus, we see how Moses' utter dependence on his God for every provision changed him.

When you depend on God to fulfill a vision He has given you, your relationship with God—how you see and respond to Him—changes and changes you.

A multiplication vision shapes your closest relationships in ministry. Few people in Scripture exhibit such a noticeable focus on relationships like Paul does. Letter after letter shows us how Paul built relationships with the churches he started. Moreover, the Barnabas > Paul > Timothy powerhouse is one of our strongest examples of mentoring in Scripture. Paul knew his relationships were vital to advancing the gospel. When we pursue a God-given vision, like-minded people with the same passions and goals inevitably cross our paths. Our opportunities to influence and be influenced by high-capacity leaders increase, and we begin to seek out and spend time with people who have our heart for movement and Kingdom focus. Your relationships will change you.

A multiplication vision shapes your priorities. Having a vision keeps us laser-focused. When opportunities come our way with no clear connection to multiplication, it's an easy "no." A clear vision provides us with a filter through which we can run every idea, opportunity and decision. Vision gives you a picture of an unrealized future and the guardrails you need to stay on the path.

A Vision for Multiplication Changes Your Church

Multipliers can tell story after story of how they've seen their church transform as a result of their focus on a vision beyond their backyard, city and state.

Casting a clear, compelling vision that calls your church to a specific purpose and mobilizes people into a life of mission lays the foundation for a church that thinks, acts and prays differently than a church focused only on its own growth. A church that carries out a strong multiplication vision begins to develop the characteristics of Level 5 multiplying churches. Consider some of the specific ways a multiplication vision changes your church:

Vision incubates a Kingdom-centric church. When people know and truly grasp that they are part of something bigger than themselves—something with eternal impact—they begin to be less focused on building *their* kingdom (their church) and more focused on seeing Jesus build *His* Kingdom. That means fewer tensions to navigate and more buy-in on all fronts as you pursue multiplication.

Vision nurtures a culture/community of biblical disciple making. In a church that embraces a vision for multiplication, making and multiplying disciples is paramount. Everyone in the church is a biblical disciple maker, reproducing disciples in community.

In 2016, Celebrate Community Church in Sioux Falls, South

Dakota, announced its vision for becoming a Level 5 multiplication church. Lead Pastor Keith Loy is pursuing a vision of raising up disciples within the church to become church planters who will plant fifty churches in ten years. This Level 5 vision, says Reed DeVries who serves as the "architect" for it, has "transformed the church." Celebrate has asked a local seminary to bring training to their lay people as they plant.

"We caught the vision of Level 5," DeVries says, "and we're not going back."

Vision breeds an apostolic atmosphere. As a Multiplier, your vision for multiplication must be tied to the spectrum of APEST (Ephesians 4), which brings not only unity but also maturity in the faith. Missiologist Alan Hirsch points to the connection between APEST and a church's "sending" impulse: "When leaders begin to embrace all five giftings of the Church—apostles, prophets, evangelists, shepherds and teachers—the key value of sending and releasing becomes a natural and expected part of your church," he explains.

Vision activates your church's "sending" impulse. In a church that has a strong multiplication vision, multiplication spreads spontaneously and exponentially. People know they are called to make disciples. They know that they're part of a church that releases and sends them out to carry the gospel to every nook and cranny of society.

What would it look like if your church had a scorecard that embraced and reflected all of these values? How would things be different? How would your community transform? What would it look like for you to lead a church that's sold out to multiplication, working together for the purpose of advancing the Kingdom?

Pursuing a multiplication vision moves us toward this picture. A clear vision for multiplication is essential to every leader aspiring to become a Multiplier.

Your Pathway to Multiplication

God never wants you to stop dreaming. You should always have a vision that moves your new scorecards forward. Remember that it's not *your* vision. Whatever you pursue should be God's vision. The way by which you get to your unique multiplication vision is what we call your multiplication pathway.

A pathway is a route or way of access to a destination; a way of reaching or achieving something.[3] It connects our current reality to a more desirable future. Moving toward a future of Level 5 multiplication offers several primary pathways common to most churches. By understanding these pathways, you can learn what to expect on your multiplication journey. Throughout the rest of this chapter, we look at the most common and primary pathways to becoming a Level 5 Multiplier.

The Big Picture: Your Starting Point and Destination

When I talk about the pathways to multiplication, I like to use a GPS analogy. Because I travel quite a bit, I'm constantly relying on my smartphone to get me to where I need to go. Using specific data (my destination and current location), my phone's GPS maps a course for me. Often, the GPS will give me several pathway options. For example, I live in the suburbs of Washington, D.C. From my house to the city, I can take three different primary pathways.

To identify the different pathways, the GPS considers numerous factors including distance, time, traffic, accidents, and toll roads. At any given time, the GPS uses the unique combination of these factors to identify the best pathway. And if traffic is heavy or some other obstacle comes up, the GPS continues to make route adjustments even after I choose a primary route and start driving. In fact, often the actual pathway I use is different than the initial one.

Our journey toward multiplication is surprisingly similar. When you take inventory of your current addition-focused scorecards and then discern a new vision for where you want to go in the future, a pathway for the journey emerges.

If you've completed the free online Becoming Five assessment, you already have a pretty clear idea of your starting point and your desired destination. The assessment gives you a score (Level 1-5) and a pattern representing your past, present and future. A pattern simply gives you a snapshot of where your church has been, where you are currently, and where you'd like to go. For example, if your pattern is 2-3-4, you were a Level 2 church in the past, a Level 3 church today, and you aspire to be a Level 4 church in the future. The "3-4" numbers (your current level of multiplication and your future aspiration for multiplication) indicate your pathway. We'd say your pathway is from "3 to 4."

If you're a new church, the assessment gives you a score (1-5) reflecting your aspirational level of multiplication. Because you're new, you don't have history to establish a pattern. You'll score something like "0-0-5." This means you're a new church, and you aspire to become Level 5. Your pathway is "New to 5."

If you've taken the assessment, write your numerical pattern and descriptive pathway below (for example, "3 to 4," or "New to 5," etc.). If you've not yet taken the free assessment at becomingfive.org, stop now and complete it before you continue to the next section. It takes less than thirty minutes to finish, and results are available immediately.

My Numerical Pattern (e.g., 2-3-4): _____

My Descriptive Pathway (e.g. "3 to 4"): _____

From Pattern to Pathway

The assessment offers 125 possible different numerical patterns between 1-1-1 and 5-5-5. In *Becoming a Level Five Multiplying*

Church, I explained that we could condense these 125 patterns down to seven primary ones. As you carefully look at the differences in each of the seven patterns, you'll see unique challenges and issues for each one:

Aspiring pattern - These churches are at Level 1 and 2, but they aspire to move to Levels 4 and 5. Churches in this pattern must first internalize the value of multiplication before they can transform their behaviors.

Advancing pattern - These churches have moved from Level 1 or 2 to Level 3, and now seek to move to Level 4 or 5. They are aggressively advancing and now must overcome the strong tensions in Level 3 that can keep them in an addition-growth culture.

Breakout pattern - These churches are stuck (or happy) at Level 3. They now seek to break out to a *Reproducing pattern* - These churches have already moved from Level 3 to Level 4. They continue to feel the tensions at Level 3, yet they strongly want to continue moving toward Level 5 multiplication.

Reproducing pattern - These churches have already moved from Level 3 to Level 4. They continue to feel the tensions at Level 3, yet they strongly want to continue increasing to Level 5 multiplication.

Recovery pattern - These churches have decreased from past to present and have then increased to an aspirational score of 4 or 5—for example, a 3-2-4. Recovery pattern churches have experienced growth in their history followed by some difficulties.

Addition pattern - Churches with an addition pattern have a strong addition-growth scorecard at Level 3. Possibly caught in the grip of addition culture, they have not yet embraced a future aspiration for multiplication.

Survivor pattern - The "future" score of churches with this pattern points to Level 2. These churches may be struggling and have difficulty seeing beyond survival thinking, thus the low score on their aspirations.

Churches with *Addition* or *Survivor* patterns are just flat out not aspiring to Levels 4 and 5. They are either stuck or happy with their current level of multiplication. To move toward multiplication, they must first undergo a transformation in their values and vision to establish a sincere desire for multiplication. If that kind of revolutionary shift happens, the multiplication pattern will change to reflect one of the other five patterns. If not, they will remain stuck at their current levels.

The other patterns for existing churches, plus the "0-0-4" and "0-0-5" patterns for new churches, represent the core patterns for multiplication. We can express these patterns as one of six different "pathways" to multiplication. The six pathways to multiplication include:

Core pathways

- Level 3 to 4
- Level 4 to 4+
- New to 4
- New to 5
- Level 1 or 2 to 4

Derivative pathways - These pathways either "derive" or find their context using specific elements of the core pathways; or they are pathways we have yet to fully understand and discover:

- Levels 1, 2, 3, or 4 to 5

In *Dream Big, Plan Smart*, we fully describe each of these pathways, including key characteristics and tensions. My hope is you'll carefully explore each description and come away from with a clear understanding of each pathway and the insight you'll need to follow it toward multiplication.

Our supplementary free eBooks, *Dream Big Questions* and *Dream Big Workbook,* are designed to guide you through the details of developing a written vision for multiplication. *Dream Big Workbook* includes more than twenty practical tools to help you. Be sure to take advantage of these free resources.

Hopefully, you're feeling equipped with the knowledge and insight needed to change your personal scorecard and your church's current scorecard; develop new scorecards for multiplication; and identify a vision and pathway for implementing and advancing your church's scorecard with your team and in your church.

Armed with a vision for multiplication, your next step is to get serious and begin to create a multiplication culture that permeates and embeds your vision into the DNA of your church. Without it, vision and pathways are nothing more than cool-sounding concepts that we dream and talk about, yet never put into action.

Putting It into Practice

• *If the Church's mission is disciple making ("go and make disciples"), what is Jesus' vision for the Church? How does this vision relate to healthy church multiplication?*

• *What is your current vision for your church? How big is your dream? What are the three to five core elements of your vision?*

• *Are your senior leaders and staff aligned with the vision? To what degree?*

• *What evidence do you have that this vision is leading to action and progress in the right direction? What specific progress have you made in the past year? As Ephesians 4 describes, are you becoming more united as a faith community with each passing year? Are you reaching increasing levels of maturity and fullness in Jesus?*

• *Play out your current vision path and direction for five, ten or even twenty years. What is your church on track to accomplish in that timeframe, and who is it on track to become?*

• *Why is it important to understand core pathways before starting the planning process?*

Tools for Multipliers

New to Five: Starting a Level 5 Multiplying Church by Ralph Moore and Jeff Christopherson. This is the first book in Exponential's series exploring the primary pathways to multiplication. In it, Level 5 Multiplier Ralph Moore gives us an inside look at the Hope Chapel movement (2,300 churches and counting), sharing stories and transferrable principles to tell us how he has started churches at Level 5. Jeff Christopherson, who oversees The Send Network, plays the role of commentator throughout the book, adding his learned insights from planting churches and now working with thousands of church planters.

Beyond 4: Leading Your Church Toward Level 5 Multiplication by Tim Hawks and Larry Walkemeyer. Our second book in the "Pathways" series includes a wealth of insight for what it takes to travel the 4 to 4+ multiplication pathway. Level 4+ Multipliers Tim and Larry vividly share their stories of climbing beyond the basecamp of Level 4 toward the summit of Level 5 multiplication. In addition to their inspiring experiences, they bring the practical lessons they've learned along the way.

Dream Big Workbook by Will Mancini offers several Vision Exercises to help you and your team define and refine your church's vision for multiplication. Use these exercises to prompt and guide your vision process.

Chapter 12
Multiplication Culture

They devoted themselves to the apostles' teaching and to fellowship, to the breaking of bread and to prayer. Everyone was filled with awe at the many wonders and signs performed by the apostles. All the believers were together and had everything in common. They sold property and possessions to give to anyone who had need. Every day they continued to meet together in the temple courts. They broke bread in their homes and ate together with glad and sincere hearts, praising God and enjoying the favor of all the people. And the Lord added to their number daily those who were being saved
(Acts 2:42-47).

When our conviction so perfectly lines up with our practices (like what we read about in Acts chapter 2), God's response is growth. It becomes the inevitable outcome. As a result, we pass a tipping point where our core convictions, our stories, and our practices are so strongly aligned with who we are that we actually have to try *not* to grow.

Pause and reflect on the culture we read about in Acts 2:42-47. What were their core values and convictions that shaped their stories and practices? Now think about the stories they told one another. Imagine the power of the stories that started with, "I remember when Jesus ... ." The wonders and events this community of believers experienced in practice perfectly aligned with the teaching they received.

This combination resulted in two key outcomes that apply to most all strong cultures. First, "insiders," those who are part of the community or cause, become more fully devoted, raving fans of the cause. You might say they become owners in the crusade. The description in Acts uses the word "devoted." Devotion is the fuel of any movement. As people buy into the culture, devotion increases. Second, "outsiders," those not yet part of the community or cause, see what the insiders have and want it.

A powerfully aligned culture increases the devotion of insiders and fuels the addition of outsiders to join the cause. From Apple to Starbucks to your favorite local restaurant, every organization has a culture. You can't stop it. It's what you become known for, and it powerfully shapes the way you see the world and the decisions you make.

As a Multiplier, your role in stewarding and cultivating culture may be the most important one you play. Value survival, and you'll establish a scarcity (subtraction) culture. Value addition growth, and you'll establish an accumulation culture. Value multiplication, and you'll establish a sending culture.

In a 2015 article for *Forbes* magazine, Southwest Airlines Founder Herb Kelleher says the unique core of any company's success is the most difficult thing for others to imitate—not their products, services or unique strategies, but rather the distinctive culture that penetrates and shapes everything they do.[1]

Defining and Building Culture

While culture is notoriously difficult to define, leadership consultant Samuel Chand says the best way to understand it is through the statement: *This is how we do things here.*

"Culture is the prevalent attitude. It is the collage of spoken and unspoken messages," he says.[2]

So how do we get to this tipping point where we begin to see our churches shift from working hard to multiply to a place where reproduction is just a natural part of their DNA? How do you as a leader aspiring to become a Multiplier start to make the shift to a powerfully aligned culture that embeds your vision for your new multiplication-based scorecards, both in you and in your church?

Throughout this chapter, we'll be answering those questions. Specifically, we'll focus on how we align our core convictions with our practices in such ways that over time, we find ourselves sharing our own reproducing stories and reveling in the fruit of a culture of radical multiplication.

When our conviction to be leaders who multiply others so perfectly lines up with our practices like what we read about in Acts, God's response is multiplication. It becomes the inevitable outcome. As a result, we pass a tipping point where our core convictions, our story and our practices are so strongly aligned with who we are that, like Ed Stetzer and Warren Bird say in their book, *Viral Churches*, we actually have to try *not* to multiply.[3]

The two researchers pinpoint only one thing that needs to happen for church multiplication to become mainstream: "You need to do it!" they write.[4] In other words, multiplication must be both a core conviction and part of your practice (for example, planting a church before buying a building; sending staff to plant; or supporting a church rather than keeping staff, etc.). At this point in your journey, do your practices as a leader and a church reflect what you say are your core convictions? What are your practices saying about your scorecards and how you're defining success both personally and in your church?

The Foundations of a Powerfully Aligned Culture

Every culture regardless of its context shares these common elements:

- a unique and distinctive set of core values;
- a unique language and narrative that continually celebrates and communicates those values;
- clear expectations, practices and behaviors that bring those values to life in tangible ways for people. People need to hear you say it in a way that makes sense and inspires action, and then see you doing what you say.

When we have strong alignment and synergy between these three elements, we start to create a specific culture. Missing just one of the three elements will sabotage your multiplication vision. These three elements of culture function like the tiny wheel weights that keep your car tires balanced. If any of the three get even slightly out of alignment, you'll feel the negative impact to multiplication.

Each culture is unique and emerges from the burdens, passions and experiences that God places in your heart. The most effective cultures powerfully align their core values, language and expected behaviors, or practices in a manner that builds trust and devoted followers, and makes it simple for people to participate personally. When people easily get it and want to be part of it, you embed your vision and move your scorecards forward. Alignment of the pieces helps people know what you're about and that you are serious enough about it that your words translate to action and impact.

The model we're using for the basic elements of a powerfully aligned culture comes from leadership and culture strategist Brian Zehr. Brian loves the church, works with numerous organizations and has experience working on staff helping lead a national church-planting network.

In the diagram below, Zehr illustrates the importance of culture and how values, narrative and behaviors must align to form a powerful culture. Let's take a deeper look into each of these elements.

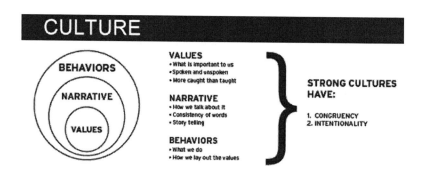

Culture Element 1: Values and Core Convictions

Zehr says that we can discern our true values by asking the question: What is the most important thing we need to be doing or that we are about right now? What is important enough to us that it transcends all we do and shapes how we do what we do?

"I always say that if I go visit a church three or four weeks in a row, I can tell what's actually most important [to them]," Zehr says. "I can tell by how they interact with each other, by what things are and aren't prioritized in their ministries. I can tell whether or not living on mission is important. I can tell if they care about the community. So, more is caught from them than is actually taught."

Values are deeply embedded and shape how a local church does everything they do. You see it, you hear it, and you feel it. Values are like a magnetic force field surrounding the people and operations of the church, proactively shaping the things to come and correcting the things that go off track. In the diagram above, the center circle represents values because they bring life, meaning and context to the other elements of narrative and behavior. The clarity of your narrative/language and your behavior/practices is an overflow of the clarity and conviction of your values.

As I mentioned earlier, prior to entering full-time ministry I spent many years as an engineer at the U.S. Division of Naval Reactors. We were responsible for all aspects of nuclear propulsion in navy ships, including reactor and system design, operation, maintenance, repair and dismantling of reactor systems. The standards were stringent and the safety record unblemished. On the occasion of our 50th anniversary and in achieving over 100 million miles powered in nuclear ships, dignitaries from around the world sent their congratulations.

The vice president of the United States asked, "What is the secret of excellence in the Naval Reactors organization?" Without hesitation, our director said, "Excellence is a concept [value] so deeply engrained in whom we are that the word never needs to be used." I remember hearing that and thinking, *Wow, I don't remember ever hearing the word. I need to think about what it even means.*

Our record to outsiders shouted "excellence!" It's what we became known for based on the results we achieved. But we never sat around talking about excellence. Instead, we demonstrated it in everything we did—from the small things to the huge decisions. Excellence didn't happen overnight or through one act or decision, but emerged through the disciplined, consistent application of language and behaviors that were perfectly aligned to our core values.

Currently, the average person would not look at churches on *Outreach* magazine's latest Top 100 Largest and Fastest-Growing lists and ask the leaders of those churches, "What is the secret to your multiplication?" Instead they would ask questions like, "What is the secret to your growth?" or "What is the secret to your innovation?" or "How did you break the 500-growth barrier?"

Multipliers value multiplication, trusting numerical growth will happen as a byproduct.

The questions outsiders ask based on what they see, hear, and experience give us the best insights into what our actual values are. Not what we want them to be, but what they actually are. Pause and reflect on the questions that outsiders would most likely ask about your church. Be honest. What core values are bleeding through to the language and practices or behaviors that people see, feel and hear? Would they ask, "What is the secret to your multiplication?"

If not, go ahead and ask yourself another honest question: "How strong is my conviction to be a multiplying church?" Do you want it, or is it just a nice concept? Are you willing to put to death the deeply embedded addition-growth scorecards that shape the prevailing definition of success in the U.S. Church and its leaders? If so, that story must start with multiplication becoming one of your most important core values.

Culture Element 2: Narratives

Let's revisit Southwest Airlines. To effectively reinforce their values, the company uses storytelling. Says Southwest CEO Gary Kelly: "Storytelling is the single most effective way to remind employees of the company's purpose and to reinforce the purpose in their day-to-day interactions with customers."[5] To tell their story, every week Kelly gives a "shout out"—public praise—to employees who have gone above and beyond to show great customer service. And each month Southwest's *Spirit* magazine features the story of a deserving employee.

Our real core values shape and define our language and our narratives—*how* we talk about what matters most to us. This is why "outsiders" or visitors can discern so much about our true values in one visit to our churches.

If your church says one of your core values is caring about the surrounding community, then the language you're using to naturally describe that care should indicate your convictions. Do the people in your church talk about inclusiveness and building relationships in the community? Or is the conversation more about simply giving money to various community efforts? Do you integrate regular stories of community engagement and impact in your sermons, newsletters, and printed materials, etc.?

In life, we tend to talk about and get most excited about the things we care most about. It's the "twinkle in the eye" and "pep in the step" effect. These things shape our language and our practices. They most naturally reflect our passions or burdens. Our passion and burdens provide a direct lens into our values.

I've already talked about Bob Buford as a hero maker. I have the privilege of working alongside Bob, founder of Leadership Network (leadnet.org) and Halftime (halftimeinstitute.org). For more than twenty-five years, Bob was mentored by modern management pioneer Peter Drucker. Inevitably, in virtually every conversation Bob and I have, Peter Drucker's name comes up. Bob will lean forward with a twinkle in his eye, and newfound vibrancy in his voice and say, "I remember when Peter said ... ." Bob can't help it. His core values and convictions naturally overflow to shape and define his language and narrative.

Pause and reflect on your church's language and narrative. Are there specific themes or patterns? What core values do the stories reflect? Are there core values you publicly state, but if you're honest you don't have the stories to bring them to life?

Brian Zehr offers this caution: "I remember when a church I was working with told me their key value was life-changing relationships with God. But when I asked to hear a recent story about someone whose life was changed, leaders could only recall stories from decades ago. This church was either suffering from wishful values, or not living out their values."

There is also real danger in forcing language and storytelling that doesn't line up with your real core values. In our zeal to be or project something that we're not, we risk being perceived as disingenuous or shallow. People will see through and pick up on our integrity by looking at our words and actions. Does what we say (or don't say) line up with what we do (or don't do)? Your language and narrative are key components in helping move people from *knowing* your core values (the first element) to actively *participating* in what you do (the third element discussed below).

Once our core values and language are aligned, then we have to ensure our practices, behaviors, and decisions also line up.

Culture Element 3: Behaviors, Practices and Decisions

The third element of culture is where you might say, "the rubber meets the road." You can have perfect values and a great narrative, but if your behaviors and practices are inconsistent with the story you tell, you'll struggle. Your behaviors and practices will always be self-correcting and align to your *real* values and story.

Our words can say that we are a lean, fit and healthy athlete. But the food we eat, our weight, and our blood pressure reading tell the real story. The results and outcomes, and the behaviors that produce them, are the proof of our real values. They tell the real story.

At my friend Dan Smith's Momentum Christian Church, people continually hear about the scorecard of sending and naturally begin to ask themselves what it will look like for them to be sent. The language and practices naturally help people to transition from "if" to "when" as they take ownership for the cause.

We must seek to powerfully and simply link the language and narrative we use with the behaviors and actions we want people to take. And that process must be simple. From our initial review of multiplication-growth cultures, it appears they tend to be far more simple and reproducible than the addition-growth strategies that are always reliant on the next leading-edge idea or innovation.

Deliberately and frequently pause to assess whether or not the things you're doing are congruent with the values you espouse and the narrative you tell. Then proactively look for and find stories, metaphors and language that reinforce whom you want to be.

For example, if you value personal evangelism, be careful about how you celebrate the results of direct mail marketing campaigns. Rather than celebrating the impersonal activity or action of direct mail and the resulting new people showing up at church, find and celebrate stories of church members who used the direct mail card to invite their neighbor to church. Same action, but different narrative. Consider creating a similar matrix/schedule of powerful stories that bring to life how your core values are translating into action.

Language and narratives help the "outsider" who experiences your church become an "insider," easily taking ownership of the process and then bringing along other outsiders on the journey. The cycle easily repeats when the language and the practices are tightly integrated.

Culture-Defining Questions and Decisions

Most of our tensions and the resulting practices we put in place in response to them find their roots in a handful of key questions that play a vital role in shaping the culture you create in your church.

Brett Andrews, leader of New Life Christian Church in Chantilly, Virginia, faced many of these tensions. Brett was called to plant a church and like many planters, he started with just his wife and practically no money or expertise. He had more questions than answers, but he also had a conviction to lead a church-planting church that would be faithful with the few resources under its care—trusting that God would bless with even more.

Brett had no idea what it meant or what it would take to be a church-planting church. But again, he had passion and conviction. After three years of struggle in the survival culture, New Life took a deep breath and celebrated being financially self-sufficient. The journey wasn't easy. Brett tells of the seasons when he was unsure whether or not anyone would show up the next week, or if his family would have money for food. Like most planters, he lost some of his closest friends who left the launch team. So that deep breath of celebration came at a deep cost and with great struggle.

But also with that deep breath came a number of defining moments: "Would they buy land and build? Or plant their first church? Would they take care of their own internal family's needs to care for the 99 safe sheep? Or would they risk everything and go after the one lost sheep? Would they let go and send their best staff? Or hold on to them tightly?"

To plant their first church, New Life chose to release two of their three staff members and a significant portion of their budget, rather than follow the conventional path of building a facility. After all, facilities help legitimize your existence. In retrospect, that one decision set the course for the leader and church Brett and New Life would become. From that point on, the church has gone on to be involved in more than one hundred church plants, has founded several church-planting support ministries, and has even helped start Exponential.

There is a good chance you've never heard of Brett. The scorecards of Multipliers don't land you on the Top 100 lists. But pause and imagine the impact of New Life not making that one decision. Had they waited until the elusive day when the resources lined up correctly to plant churches, their impact would now be measured primarily by their addition rather than their multiplication. Momentum Church's Dan Smith is a church planter out of Brett's church. Dan started the church with a vision of sending out one hundred-plus leaders to plant or be part of planting teams. Where would those one hundred leaders be now if Brett had chosen to build a building rather than plant their first church? The chain reaction of multiplication is profound.

The bottom line is that we can't establish a multiplication growth culture without bucking conventional thinking and making some radical decisions. How prepared are you? Are you willing to:

- Plant your first church before building or buying your first building?
- Send your first church planter before accumulating your first two to three staff members?
- Commit the first fruits of your financial resources, tithing 10 percent or more to church multiplication, even before paying other essentials like salaries?
- Plant your first church before starting your first multisite?
- Come alongside and coach other planters in your area who can benefit from your encouragement and experience?

- Start or join a church-planting network, locally or nationally, to collaborate with others, find accountability for multiplying and building a multiplication culture, and get involved in more than you otherwise could?

Moving Forward

Knowing how culture is created and nurtured allows us to look ahead to the predictable tensions you'll inevitably face in putting a multiplication growth culture in place. For example, if your church commits to a $6 million building campaign before it plants a church, what does that say about your priorities? Or if you call yourself a multiplying leader but continue adding more staff before you train and release a church planter, what are you modeling for your church?

Most of these key decisions draw defining boundaries around the specific culture you create: The beautiful new building you want will give you momentum and accelerate growth. The best staff members will help you break the next growth barrier. The new site will help you expand the number of services your church offers.

These decisions are the right ones for addition growth, but we simply need to understand that those decisions can also become the barriers that keep us from creating a multiplication culture and the right macro-level strategies. Remember, our actions define our real values. The best spin or marketing campaign in the world can't change that.

In the next chapter, we'll look at the three types of primary tensions you'll face in seeking to move beyond addition thinking to multiplication thinking. Be prepared. This is a dangerous journey and will require you to put to death some of the things you've grown to idolize. Overcoming these tensions as you create and implement a culture and new scorecards that value and champion multiplication will take courage, persistence and intentionality.

Putting It into Practice

• *What culture are you creating in your church? Scarcity/survival, addition, multiplication? What culture have you become known for?*

• *Why is culture creation your most important role as a Multiplier?*

• *To create a multiplication culture, what are the specific behaviors deeply engrained in your culture that you'll need to overcome and change?*

• *In 20 years, what specific behaviors (that you're not currently practicing today) would you like to see embedded into your church's DNA?*

• *Pause and reflect on your church's language and narrative. Are there specific themes or patterns? What core values do the stories reflect? Are there core values you publicly state, but if you're honest don't have the stories to bring them to life?*

Tools for Becoming Multipliers

Spark: Igniting a Culture of Multiplication in Your Church by Todd Wilson. The first in Exponential's series of multiplication-focused eBooks, *Spark* thoroughly explores what culture is and why it's important to embedding your multiplication vision; the cultures that prominent church cultures leaders most naturally create; and how culture is created.

Give God Some Credit: Risk Taking for Future Impact by Brett Andrews. Brett candidly shares the story of New Life Christian Church's unimaginable impact, including the struggles and worries. Brett's story of how he became a church Multiplier offers poignant reminders that even though we can't see God working in or lives and ministry, He is indeed, as Brett says, "working upstream."

Sending Church: Stories of Momentum and Multiplication by Dan Smith. On paper, Momentum's just a regular church. For their first nine years, they averaged 250 or less people. But the numbers don't tell the whole story. Led by Multiplier Dan Smith, the church has created a strong sending culture to reach more broken people through new churches.

Intentional Culture training video featuring Brian Zehr. From establishing a healthy, multiplying culture from the start and protecting it once your church is planted, culture strategist Brian Zehr fleshes out intentional steps to help you move from survival to multiplication.

Create a Multiplying Culture in Your Church: 6 Practical Steps podcast with Brian Bloye. West Ridge church planter Brian Bloye draws from his experience as a Multiplier to share practical and doable steps for creating a multiplying culture.

Chapter 13
Multiplication Barriers

... In this world, you will have trouble ... Jesus (John 16:33).

Jesus' words to His disciples offer us specific truth that you can take to heart as you pursue becoming a Multiplier and your new multiplication-based scorecard. It's not simply an option or possibility. Tension in our lives is unavoidable.

I don't have to tell you that church leaders aren't immune to trouble or that churches also live in a constant state of tension. As a key element of Jesus' strategy against Satan, why would we expect anything less? Regardless of whether a church is a Level 1 or Level 5 or somewhere in between, the tensions it experiences can distract and keep it from being and becoming what the Founder intends.

That doesn't change the fact that we try as hard as we can to avoid tension, conquer it, or make it go away.

Don't miss this important truth: *No matter what level of multiplication you find yourself at, you WILL have tension.* Nothing you do will allow you to reach a level of multiplication that is tension-free. The Level 1 church that lives in a scarcity culture will not suddenly find itself tension-free when it graduates to a Level 3 church. The tensions will simply shift to new ones.

So the key questions for you are not, "Will we have tension?" or "How do I avoid tension?" The game changer is how you leverage tension to grow and more deeply embed a culture of multiplication. The profound, transformative question is always, "How do we leverage the behaviors of multiplying churches to help us maneuver and grow in this current season of tension?"

The Magnetic Force of Tensions

Recall our integrated picture of the cultures that are core to the five levels of multiplication:

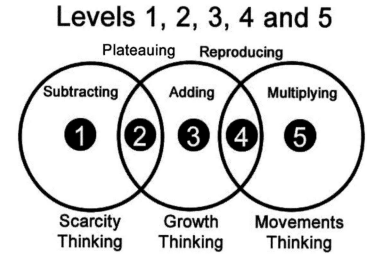

Now, consider what would happen if we placed a strong magnet to the left of Level 1. For this illustration, assume your church is now a metal object in the Level 1 circle.

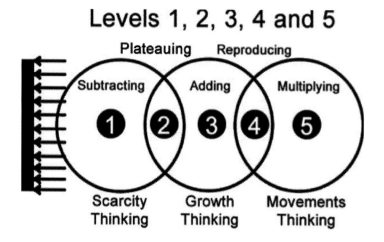

Now think about a magnet. The closer you get to it, the stronger its attractive force. When you're a foot away, you don't even feel its force. The diagram above shows that the farther you move to the right (toward Level 2 and higher), the less you feel the subtraction magnet. Here's the corollary: The closer you get to a magnet's force field, the stronger the force and the tougher it becomes to break free of its grip.

In this illustration, the force field near the magnet represents the culture you create in your church. If you create a survival culture, you'll constantly experience the tension of scarcity that's drawing you toward subtraction.

Leaders that do break free to Level 2 begin to experience the force field of the addition magnet (see the next graphic).

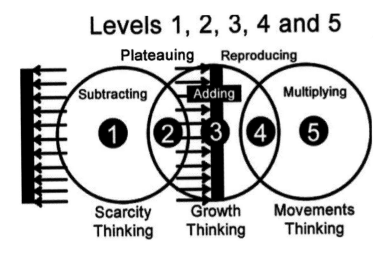

In a culture driven by our addition-focused scorecards, the addition magnet is very strong. As you move toward it, the magnet's force becomes increasingly powerful and even addictive. I've previously described the journey of a Level 3 Multiplier as the continuing process of conquering the next growth barrier. This Level 3 magnet is at the center of addition-growth, drawing you closer and closer.

Leaders in the Level 2 region feel the effects of both the subtraction and the addition magnets.

For example, a church growing toward eighty-plus people in the traditional paradigm will hit a growth ceiling (due to staffing capacity) when it reaches eighty to one hundred people—exactly in the range of the average U.S. church size. Leaders conclude they need to "add" staff to "grow." Unfortunately, their paradigm becomes, "We can't add staff *until* we grow. We can't afford it."

So today's paradigms/models ("paid staff do the heavy lifting" and "we can only do what we can financially afford") actually self-sabotage, paralyzing a church at fewer than one hundred people. Leaders become caught in the tension between the subtraction and addition culture magnets (tensions).

The impact is even more pronounced in Level 3 Multipliers that want to break free of the addition magnet's grip and move to Levels 4 and 5. The graphic below is spot on. The same strong magnet (or culture) that pulls a church into greater levels of addition-growth is the very one that keeps it from moving to greater levels of multiplication.

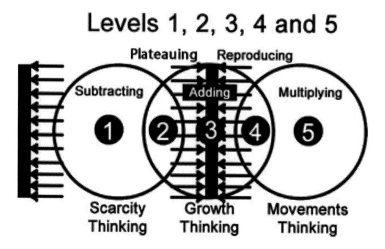

Levels 1, 2, 3, 4 and 5

Plateauing   Reproducing

Subtracting   Adding   Multiplying

1   **2**   **3**   **4**   **5**

Scarcity   Growth   Movements
Thinking   Thinking   Thinking

Specifically, the addition strategies used to conquer the progressive growth barriers in Level 3 include things like large, growing specialty staff; facilities with large mortgage debt; organizational/structural complexity required to manage numerous ministries and sites; and a huge demand for volunteers and strong volunteer leaders, etc.

The financial and leadership resources required to get a church to Level 3 are the same resources needed to fuel multiplication in Levels 4 and 5. When this tyranny of the *or* emerges, addition-growth usually wins out over multiplication. The practices and behaviors required in Levels 4 and 5 always seem to be in tension with the allocation of resources to fuel what has already been built in Level 3. The addition magnet (culture) simply overpowers most churches (and their leaders) that desire increasing levels of multiplication.

There is another magnet (see below) to the right of Level 5. This one is built into the intended DNA of the church by its Founder. Unfortunately, most leaders are so captive to the addition culture in Level 3 that they never get close enough to the multiplication magnet to see its force field overtake the embedded addition culture.

As leaders venture beyond their current walls and reproduce sites (campuses), they functionally press into Level 4 practices. However, most current multisite activity is rooted in Level 3 addition rather than Level 5 multiplication (multisite as a multiplication strategy has yet to be demonstrated).

Putting It Into Perspective

As a linear progression, most U.S. churches are born into Levels 1 or 2, but as we've said earlier, few (less than 0.05 percent) ever make it to Level 5. Overcoming the subtraction magnet (culture) and then the addition magnet (culture) are major challenges. The normal path is linear with progression from Level 1 to 2 to 3 to 4 to 5. It's like a funnel with 80 percent at one end and virtually 0 percent making it to the other end.

Here are several summary truths about tensions to consider and embrace:

- Most churches are born into Level 1 or 2. The subtraction or scarcity culture is a strong shaping factor that can hold churches captive to decision making that's rooted in survival thinking. Some percent of leaders are at Levels 1 and 2.

- Approximately 16 percent of leaders find themselves moving toward Level 3 addition-growth. The Level 3 addition magnet is extremely powerful. It fosters a culture that aligns most everything the church does to addition strategies. If Level 3 leaders are not intentional about multiplying, they may unintentionally replace the target of making biblical disciples with addition-growth.

- Approximately 4 percent of leaders put some Level 4 practices in place. However, the Level 3 addition magnet is so strong that these leaders have a difficult time breaking free from addition culture's grip, and many continue functioning with Level 3 behaviors.

- Less than 0.05 percent of U.S. church leaders are Level 5 Multipliers. By leaning into multiplication and putting Level 5 practices into place, we will increasingly expose ourselves to the multiplication magnet that's embedded, but suppressed, within the church's DNA.

No matter where you currently find yourself, you can choose to put Level 5 multiplication practices in place; maybe not all at once, but one step at a time. Revolutionary change starts with courageous leaders who are willing to embrace new scorecards rooted in the values of multiplication, characterized by the practices of Level 5 leaders and churches, and squarely focused on making and mobilizing disciples on mission.

Deceptions and Spiritual Warfare

As Scripture tells us, Satan is a master at deception. He came to "steal, kill and destroy" (John 10:10). His schemes are powerfully present in the dynamics that distract us from becoming the Level 5 Multipliers we were made to be. He continually whispers lies into our thoughts, often seeking to feed off the unhealthy attributes of our personal scorecards. We buy into the lies and begin thinking and acting with the scarcity and growth biases of Levels 1, 2, and 3 profiles, rather than the generous and abundant behaviors of Levels 4 and 5.

Satan is particularly good at introducing confusion that keeps us distracted. He knows that movements are fueled by Level 5 churches, so he simply needs to keep us consumed at Levels 1, 2, and 3. With 80 percent of U.S. churches at Levels 1 and 2, 4 percent at Level 4 and fewer than 0.05 percent at Level 5, it appears he is doing his job of keeping us distracted—via two simultaneous deceptions:

- First, he confuses our motives and our scorecards. Instead of embracing more biblical scorecards of multiplication characterized by making biblical disciples, and sending/releasing leaders to multiply, we adopt the sexier Level 3 scorecards of accumulation and consumption. We embrace the wrong personal scorecard and scorecard for our church.

- Second, he paralyzes us at Levels 1, 2, and 3 by keeping us captive to the cultures characteristic of those levels (e.g., subtraction, survival, and growth). We become so consumed and distracted within our current level that we lose sight of our intended target to make biblical disciples who make disciples that plant churches. The culture we find ourselves trapped within essentially creates a different target for us to strive for—a target characterized by attaining the winning score on a particular level. It's like getting us stuck and distracted on a specific level in a video game. Our short-term target becomes "defeating the level." As we move into Level 3, we experience a culture that's nearly impossible to overcome and defeat.

Amid these challenges, we buy into the following types of lies:

- We will [fill in the blank] when we can afford it;
- We can't [fill in the blank] until we hire another staff person, but we can't afford to hire until we grow;
- If we can just [fill in the silver bullet], we can break out of this plateau and start growing (or we can break through this next growth barrier);
- If we can get permanent facility space, then we can expand our impact;
- We will plant a church after we get stabilized and can afford it;
- Success is pioneering the latest and greatest addition-focused innovations and strategies;
- Success is breaking the next growth barrier or adding a specific number of people   within a specific period of time;
- We will get our feet wet with multisite before planting a church.

Three Common Core Tensions: Motives, Measurements and Methods

The lists of tensions you'll encounter as you implement new multiplication-focused scorecards are a mile long. However, nearly all of those tensions find their roots in three common factors: motives, measurements and methods.

Tension of motives (here or there?): *Will the church I lead (or will lead) be about my kingdom or God's Kingdom?* This tension is rooted in your definition of success. Is your vision limited to accumulating and growing larger *here* (where you are), or is it balanced with an equal focus and passion for sending *there* (the next church)?

Exponential speaker and 2/42 Community Church planter and Lead Pastor Dave Dummit cautions, "Start your 'here' (the church you're planting) with 'there' (the next church you'll plant or support) in mind. If you focus on 'there,' then 'here' will take care of itself. In that first-year phase, it's so important to get this 'here/there' tension right."

All leaders live in the tension between being *here* and *there*, with almost everything pulling them toward *here*. Having as many or more "growing there" strategies as "growing here" strategies is the difference between being a Level 3, 4, or 5 leader. Level 5 Multipliers are as passionate about *there* as they are *here*.

If you're serious about leading a reproducing, multiplying and movement-making church, then you'll have to start *here* but will need to go *there...there...there and there*! But understand, the tension between focusing *here* and going *there* will always exist.

The tension of motives is about declaring this day that multiplication matters and embracing it as a core value—not just a nice program to add on, but a value that shapes and influences your decisions, strategy, staffing, facilities, and budget. With any transition to a new core value comes the need for new scorecards (personal and in your church) and lens for defining and measuring success.

Tension of measurement (grow or send?): *Will this church I lead be about growing or sending?* This tension is rooted in where you prioritize your focus: Where do I focus my time, talent and treasure? Your methods (or practices and behaviors) are where you bring a multiplication culture to life. How do you balance the tension between building local capacity to grow bigger local churches, *and* building global capacity to send and release resources to start new churches? Will your primary measurement

161

of success be about your church or how many churches you can start?

Missiologist Alan Hirsch reminds us that living "sent" is not just a cool idea or term some savvy leader coined: "Being a sending church takes us to the core theology of the Church as the primary human agency of the Kingdom of God—which means there is no such thing as an "un-sent" Christian! (John 20:21, Matt. 28:19). We send because all Christians and churches are sent by God into the world."

Dave Ferguson reminds us that growth requires us to consistently ask ourselves: Will we increase seating capacity or sending capacity? "If your answer is 'sending,'" he says, "then you'll have to develop new metrics because, 'what you measure improves and what you celebrate gets repeated.'"

The word "sending" that Dave uses is the same word as the root of the word for mission (*missio* = "sent" in Latin). Our commitment to "send" measures our impact *beyond* the church, not just *in* the church.

In the tension of measurement, hard questions surface:

- How much energy are we directing toward optimizing systems at the mother church versus the amount of energy we're directing toward a system to develop leaders and staff to send to a new church plant?

- Are we hanging on to our best staff members, or sending them out as church planters?

- Are we developing our best leaders to run our programs and staff the mother church, or are we intentionally growing leaders to send them out?

- Do we have an excellent leadership residency program? Have we emphasized excellence in our leadership development/sending structures?

Level 5 Multipliers focus on sending *as much as* growing. We will never see a Level 5 multiplication movement until we're as passionate about sending as we are growing. When we embrace new scorecards focused on releasing and sending leaders, we must then rethink our addition-focused behaviors and methods to realign them with multiplication.

At this point, the conversation moves from "dream" (what we *want* to do) to practical and personal (what we *will* do). This is where courageous leadership makes all the difference. This is where the culture-shaping decisions come to life. This is where we sweat, but also where we live out our core values with integrity.

Tension of methods (safety or risk?): *Will I live out my years coasting through life, or will I take risks to do something new and to grow God's Kingdom?* At the core of this tension is how you allocate your time (activities), talents (leadership), and treasures (finances) to building local *and* Kingdom capacity. What will you actually *do*, and what hard decisions will you make to become and grow as a Multiplier? Good intentions will not move you from Level 1 to 5.

Our methods (or practices and behaviors) are where we bring a multiplication culture to life. How do we balance the tension between building local capacity to grow bigger local churches, *and* building global capacity to send and release resources to start new churches?

Three specific multiplication tensions center on actual execution and the difficult decisions leaders will need to address and resolve as they seek to build local and Kingdom capacity:

- Facilities and place
- Finances

- Relaxing versus risk-taking

Facilities and place: In the U.S. Church, one of the tensions that leaders will quickly experience is the reality of needing facilities and place: Do I build buildings or plant more churches? Do I send out my first staff before I build? Do I start a new church before I build?

Make no mistake. Buildings can be a great help to accomplishing the Great Commission. People like having a "place." Most churches see an attendance bump with new spaces. *But* they can also be a hindrance to the mission because buildings are a huge expense, costing both money and time to raise the capital. They require upkeep (more money and time), and they often create an unintended culture that focuses on *here* versus *there*.

Sending out people to plant a church before the church takes on significant building debt sends a very specific message to the church and instills a multiplication DNA. The likelihood of becoming a Level 4 or 5 multiplying church significantly increases when we choose Level 4 and 5 behaviors over Level 3 behaviors.

The building issue gives us numerous questions and decisions for us to wrestle through:

- Do we put more time into our church-planting strategy than we do into our future facility strategy?
- If we do decide that a building will move our mission forward, how will we use that platform to attract and train more leadership residents and church planters?

Level 4 and 5 leaders also live in the tension: "Do we build a building?" or "Do we plant churches?" Their bias is toward planting as they figure out the "and."

Finances: In Luke 14, Jesus tells His disciples that they will need to count the cost of following Him. For leaders that want to become Level 5 Multipliers, very real costs and risks are involved—particularly in a financial sense. Without a strong core conviction to multiply, you'll likely gravitate toward financial security instead of doing the hard work of navigating perceptions and questions. For example:

- Key givers in a church will naturally want to know the return on investment in planting new churches.
- Staff and other leaders will wonder how prioritizing the church's financial resources toward multiplication will impact their current ministries.
- Resources allocated to multiplication are not available for the local addition-growth activities that fuel attendance growth. Just like you teach your congregation to, "look at your checkbook to know your true priorities," the same is true for a church.
- Will our church at least tithe to church planting on capital campaigns and other special offerings, as well as general offerings?
- Will our church sacrifice to plant a church?
- Will our church put funds toward training church planters and developing a leadership residency?

Relaxing versus risk-taking: Many senior leaders find themselves in a comfortable place at Level 3. The financial strains of addition-growth are different than those in the survival culture of Levels 1 and 2. They have planted their church and have worked hard to grow it. Their church has grown to a certain size, and they're drawing a good salary. They are at a place in their leadership where they make more impact with less effort simply because their words have more weight now.

The questions then become:

- After working really hard for years, do I just relax now? Or do I keep taking risks?
- What about starting a network? Or a whole movement of churches?

- Am I building systems that allow me to coast/relax, or am I still engaged and taking risks?
- Am I investing myself in the next generation of church Multipliers with the same zeal I gave to conquering the Level 3 growth barriers?

At an Exponential gathering, Fellowship Monrovia Pastor Albert Tate encouraged leaders with the truth that, "God is not done with you. He has something greater for you." Drawing from the lives of Moses and Abraham, Albert pointed out that God has a reputation for tapping us on the shoulder just when we're comfortable in life and saying, "Trust Me and let's begin again!"

Navigating this tension of methods and these questions requires leaders to honestly assess their personal energy and resiliency.

Onward and Upward

In this chapter, we've highlighted the most common types of tensions you'll face in seeking to move beyond addition thinking to multiplication thinking. Be prepared. Every multiplying leader would tell you that this is a dangerous journey and will require you to put to death some of the things you've grown to idolize. Leveraging these tensions takes courage, persistence and intentionality.

One of the greatest tensions you'll face centers on sacrifice and surrender. To change the Level 3 addition-growth scorecard, you must put to death those motives, measures and methods and be a courageous change maker who bucks the old wineskins opting for new, and better, wineskins. Think of a specific tension you're currently dealing with in your church and ask yourself: *What would it look like to respond to this tension the way a Level 5 Multiplier would respond? If my future and the future of my children and their children depended on me becoming a Level 5 Multiplier, what would I do differently than what I'm doing now? What would I do with urgency?*

As a leader, one of your most difficult (and rewarding) tasks is to raise up and train other leaders—becoming a hero maker! In a multiplying church, the tension will surface: Do we send out these leaders and make heroes out of them or do we hang on to them because they help us grow our ministry (our kingdom)? Our actions speak loudly and trump our narrative.

This is what courageous leaders who value multiplication do. They lean into the future and create a new normal. They are hero-making Multipliers who take action. In the next chapter, we've outlined specific priorities with concrete short-term actions that move us toward multiplication!

Putting it Into Practice

• *Think of a specific tension you're currently dealing with in your church. What would it look like to respond to this tension the way a Level 5 Multiplier would respond?*

• *What are the "forces" pulling you to Level 3 addition?*

• *How is Satan confusing your motives and scorecard?*

• *What are the tensions keeping you from moving from "here" to "there"?*

• *Are you developing your best leaders to run your church's programs and staff the mother church, or are you intentionally growing leaders to send them out? Name five to ten people you've released and sent out in the last few years.*

• *Are you building systems that allow you to coast/relax, or are you still engaged and taking risks?*

• *Are you willing to make church multiplication a higher priority than building/expanding permanent facilities?*

• *In what ways is multisite simply an extension of adding services in your church? In what ways is it not? How might multisite be an enhancing strategy to accelerate your church's planting activities?*

Tools for Becoming Multipliers

Spark: Igniting a Culture of Multiplication by Todd Wilson. *Spark* highlights 18 different tensions that you'll face in moving from Levels 1, 2, and 3 to Levels 4 and 5.

Becoming a Level 5 Multiplying Church by Todd Wilson, Dave Ferguson and Alan Hirsch. The second anchor book in Exponential's multiplication series tackles multiplication tensions and explores how leveraging versus avoiding our tensions leads to embedded multiplication values and culture.

Becoming a Level 5 Multiplying Church online course. This free, eight-module course offers a thorough understanding of the Becoming 5 framework, including the five levels of multiplication and a comprehensive look at the tensions you'll encounter on your way toward Kingdom multiplication.

My Reproducing Plan (MRP) from Newthing Network. The MRP is a form of accountability amid addition-growth tensions as leaders dream about and commit in writing what they will do in the coming year. The MRP pulls planters away from only *here* thinking and toward *there* behaviors. Download a free copy of it at exponential.org/mrp.

Chapter 14
Moving Forward

*"Plans are only good intentions unless they immediately
degenerate into hard work."*
~ Peter F. Drucker

By now, you're fired up and inspired to create new scorecards and
become a hero-making Multiplier who advances God's Kingdom.

Over the last 13 chapters, we've looked at where we are today with
the prevailing addition-focused scorecard (the five levels of
multiplication) and the need to deconstruct it; identified the
importance of changing your personal scorecard and confronting
your misplaced motives; and discovered five essential practices for
moving from Level 1 to Level 5 leadership.

From there, we explored solid foundations for new multiplication-
based scorecards (three dimensions for multiplication); examined
why vision and a pathway for multiplication are essential for
moving your new scorecard forward; and explored your vital role
as a Multiplier in making the shift to a multiplication culture that
embeds your multiplication vision (aligning three elements of
culture); and finally, discerned the most common tensions you'll
face in the multiplication journey.

Taking Your Cue

I realize this is a lot to process. If you're feeling overwhelmed,
you're in good company. Two thousand years ago, a team of
learners felt the same way. They were grieving the loss of their
Founder and one of their twelve team members. They felt
uncertain of themselves and their future. Clearly, they were
squarely at Level 1 (subtraction culture), unable to see any
forthcoming movement.

While simply giving up would have been the easiest response, the
eleven disciples pressed on in faith, taking one small, determined

step at a time. Then Jesus showed up in Jerusalem to give them their mission—"Go!" And then, "Wait." Wait for what? They knew their assignment. What did they need to wait for?

"... wait for the gift my Father promised, which you have heard me speak about. For John baptized with water, but in a few days you will be baptized with the Holy Spirit ... you will receive power when the Holy Spirit comes on you; and you will be my witnesses in Jerusalem, and in all Judea and Samaria, and to the ends of the earth" (Acts 1:4-8).

In the first two chapters of Acts, we see how the disciples took steps to carry out Jesus' Great Commission, both before and after Pentecost. They waited for power, prayed, put the right leadership in place (Mathias replaced Judas), held to the authority of Scripture, shared the gospel, called people to action, and lived in common, modeling what they would ultimately multiply.

As leaders, we can learn from the disciples and create specific priorities with concrete short-term actions that move us toward multiplication. Like the disciples, we need to:

- rely on God's power (not ours);
- pray diligently and proactively;
- hold fervently to Jesus' commands;
- put the right leaders in place;
- call people to a higher standard;
- and model what we seek to reproduce.

Beyond Vision to Action

As you've learned by now, the pathways to Levels 4 and 5 require leaders who are intentional, courageous, and disciplined. There's a reason why only 4 percent of U.S. churches *ever* reproduce. Moving that multiplication needle requires leaders like you to face and deconstruct your current scorecard and then redefine your success via new scorecards, both for your church and for you, personally. Bottom line, becoming a Multiplier takes action.

When I hear people talk about good intentions with no plan for executing them, I always think about this quote from Peter Drucker: "Many brilliant people believe that ideas move mountains. But bulldozers move mountains; ideas show where the bulldozers should go to work."[1]

If you're serious about becoming a Multiplier that leads beyond addition, you must move beyond the inspiration of ideas or a vision. And that action needs to start right now. If you read this book and come away inspired or convicted, yet don't take specific, concrete steps to change, you won't see multiplication. It's as simple as that.

Becoming a Level 5 Multiplier who leads multiplication in and through your church *can* be a reality. Jesus doesn't ask us to do something for His purpose without empowering and equipping us with the vision and the plan for it. However, like anything in life, we can have everything we need but without action, good intentions are futile. Drucker offers another gem to remember:

"It is meaningless to speak of short-range and long-range plans," he said. "There are plans that lead to action today—and they are true plans, true strategic decisions. And there are plans that talk about action tomorrow—they are dreams, if not pretexts for non-thinking, non-planning, non-doing."[2]

Granted, we may not always have the exact blueprint in front of us. Missiologist Alan Hirsch (who contributes his insights to the eBook *Becoming a Level 5 Multiplying Church*) notes that when we commit to a vision of doing something that has never been done before, there is no blueprint or model.

"We simply have to build the bridge as we walk on it," Alan says. "And remember, no advancement or development would have ever been achieved if someone hadn't broken from the herd and charted a different (and better) way."[3]

Jesus has called you to something bigger than leading a growing church. He has called you to chart a new, inspired course. I hope by now you believe and understand that. I pray that you will take the necessary steps to become a leader who asks for the courage and wisdom to assess and deconstruct your current scorecard and then risks to establish a new definition of success, both for your church and for you, personally.

God hasn't called you to just be a leader. He has called you to be a leader who makes heroes and takes seriously His vision for multiplying biblical disciples in fresh, sometimes unconventional ways that see disciples start new communities of faith and reach into every crack and cranny of society.

He has called us to be HeroMakers and has equipped us to be Multipliers.

Putting It into Practice

• *Do you sense that God wants you to move on from your current "here" to a new "there"?*

• *Most church leaders like to dwell (or live) in the land of vision and have a difficult time moving from ideas to planning. Has this been a problem for you? How will you make sure you move from ideas to planning to action?*

• *What are the three to five most important things that you as a leader need to do in the coming year (into your next budget year) to build momentum and put your church on a trajectory in the right direction?*

• *Are you willing to commit at least 10 percent of your budget to Level 4 and 5 activities? Even if you must cut other things or step out on faith before you know where the resources will come from?*

Endnotes

Chapter 1

[1] Ed Stetzer and Warren Bird, *Viral Churches: Helping Church Planters Become Movement Makers* (Jossey-Bass, 2010).

[2] Ibid.

[3] Todd Wilson, Dave Ferguson and Alan Hirsch, *Becoming a Level 5 Multiplying Church Field Guide* (Exponential Resources, 2015).

Chapter 3

[1] Ralph Moore and Jeff Christopherson, *New to Five: Starting a Level 5 Multiplying Church* (Exponential Resources, 2017).

[2] Todd Wilson, *More: Find Your Personal Calling and Live Life to the Fullest Measure* (Zondervan, 2017).

Chapter 6

[1] Larry Walkemeyer, *Flow: Unleashing a River of Multiplication in Your Church, City and World* (Exponential Resources, 2015).

[2] Ibid.

[3] Ibid. Used by permission.

[4] Ibid.

[5] Ibid. Used by permission.

[6] Ibid. Adapted with permission.

Chapter 7

[1] Dave Ferguson and Warren Bird, *Hero Maker: 5 Essential Practices for Leaders to Multiply Leaders* (Zondervan, 2017).

Chapter 8

[1] Peter F. Drucker, Frances Hasselbein, *The Five Most Important Questions Self Assessment Tool: Participant Workshop* (Jossey-Bass, 2010), 7.

[2] Ibid.

[3] Alan Hirsch, *Disciplism: Reimaging Evangelism Through the Lens of Discipleship* (Exponential Resources, 2014).

[4] Quoted in *The Forgotten Ways: Reactivating the Missional Church* by Alan Hirsch, (Brazos Press, 2009).

Chapter 9

[1] Bob Roberts, Jr., *Real-Time Connections: Linking Your Job With God's Global Work* (Zondervan, 2010).

[2] Ibid.

Chapter 10

[1] Todd Wilson, *The Emerging Micro-Church Era: Addition, Reproduction or Multiplication* (Exponential Resources white paper, 2017).

Chapter 11

[1] Henry Blackaby, Richard Blackaby, *Experiencing God* (B & H Publishing Group, 2014).

[2] Henry Blackaby, Richard Blackaby, *Spiritual Leadership: Moving People on to God's Agenda* (B & H Publishing Group, 2013).

[3] definition of pathway, thefreedictionary.com/pathway.

Chapter 12

[1] Carmine Gallo, "Southwest Airlines Motives Employees With a Bigger Purpose Than a Paycheck," (*Forbes* magazine, January 21, 2014).

[2] Samuel Chand, *Cracking Your Church's Culture Code* (Jossey-Bass, 2010).

[3] Ed Stetzer and Warren Bird, *Viral Churches: Helping Church Planters Become Movement Makers* (,).

[4] Ibid.

[5] Carmine Gallo, "Southwest Airlines Motives Employees With a Bigger Purpose Than a Paycheck," (*Forbes* magazine, January 21, 2014).

Chapter 14

[1] Peter Drucker, *Managing Oneself* (Harvard Business Press, 2008).

[2] Peter Drucker, *The Practice of Management* (HarperBusiness Reissue edition, 2006)

[3] Todd Wilson, Dave Ferguson and Alan Hirsch, *Becoming a Level 5 Multiplying Church Field Guide* (Exponential Resources, 2015).

Related Multiplication Resources

FREE eBooks

20+ new free eBooks are in our multiplication library. Authors include J.D. Greear, Ralph Moore, Larry Walkemeyer, Bruce Wesley, Tim Hawks, K.P. Yohannan, Ajai Lall, Brian Bolt, Jeff Leake, and many more. These leaders of multiplying churches share their journey of creating a sending culture of multiplication.

These eBooks are in addition to 60+ existing free eBooks in Exponential's resource library. Check out exponential.org/resource-ebooks to download these books.

Exponential Conferences

Don't miss the opportunity to gather with like-minded church multiplication leaders at Exponential's 2018 events:

Exponential National | Orlando, Florida | Feb 26 – March 1, 2018 | 1000s of leaders, 150+ speakers, 150+ workshops, 40 simultaneous workshop tracks, and 12 Preconference Labs.

Exponential Regionals bring the full punch of the national event theme in a shorter duration and more intimate gathering that helps leaders save on travel expenses. Regionals take place in Washington, D.C., Chicago IL, Southern California, Northern California, and Houston TX.

Visit exponential.org/events to learn more.

FREE Online Multiplication Assessment

Discover your church's level of multiplication via our free online tool. It only takes 20 minutes to complete and is available at becomingfive.org. A total of 6 Free tools are being made available.

FREE Online Multiplication Courses

The Becoming Five Course and Dream Big Course are designed to delve deeper into the practical elements of church multiplication. Leaders wanting to multiply their church will find valuable training in the form of audio, video, and written content supplied by dozens of multiplying practitioners, with the ability to work at their own pace. Visit exponential.org/register/b5-course/ to register.

Digital Access Passes (Training Videos)

Exponential offers downloadable content from all 10 main stage sessions via our Digital Access Pass (a separate pass for each conference theme) at exponential.org/digital-access-pass/:

2015: "SPARK: Igniting a Culture of Multiplication"

2016: "Becoming a Level 5 Multiplying Church"

2017: "Dream Big: Discover Your Pathway to Level 5 Multiplication"

2018: "HeroMaker: Becoming a Level 5 Multiplier"

Connect with Exponential on Social Media:

Twitter - @churchplanting
Facebook - Facebook.com/churchplanting
Instagram – Instagram.com/church_planting
RSS - http://feeds.feedburner.com/exponential

Other FREE Exponential Resources on Multiplication

The following eBooks are available for free download via exponential.org/resource-ebooks/

Dream Big, Plan Smart: Discovering Your Pathway to Level 5 Multiplication by Todd Wilson and Will Mancini

Dream Big Workbook by Will Mancini and Todd Wilson

Dream Big Questions by Todd Wilson and Bill Couchenour

Becoming a Level Five Multiplying Church by Todd Wilson and Dave Ferguson with Alan Hirsch

Spark: Igniting a Culture of Multiplication by Todd Wilson

Becoming a Disciple Maker: The Pursuit of Level 5 Disciple Making by Bobby Harington and Greg Wiens

New to Five: Starting a Level 5 Multiplying Church by Ralph Moore and Jeff Christopherson

Beyond 4: Leading Your Church toward Level 5 Multiplication by Larry Walkemeyer and Tim Hawks

The Emerging Micro-Church Era: Addition, Reproduction, or Multiplication by Todd Wilson

Play Thuno: The World-Changing Multiplication Game by Larry Walkemeyer

Sending Capacity, Not Seating Capacity by J.D. Greear and Mike McDaniel

Multipliers: Leading Beyond Addition

Launch Strong: A Planning Guide for Launching a Multiplying Church by Brett Andrews and Dale Spaulding

You Can Multiply Your Church: One Journey to Radical Multiplication by Ralph Moore

Flow: Unleashing a River of Multiplication in Your Church, City and Word by Larry Walkemeyer

The Journey: Toward a Healthy Multiplying Church by Darrin Patrick

Collaboration for Multiplication: The Story of the Houston Church Planting Network by Bruce Wesley

Sending Church: Stories of Momentum and Multiplication by Dan Smith

Together for the City: What Can Happen When the Mission is Bigger than 1 Congregation by Tom Hughes and Kevin Haah

Saturating Austin: A Strategy as Big as Your City by Tim Hawks and John Herrington

Igniting Movements: Multiplying Churches in Dark Places by Dr. Ajai Lall and Josh Howard

Reach: A Story of Multiplication in the City by Brian Bolt

More Than BBQ: How God is Creating a City-Wide Church Planting Movement in Kansas City by Dan Southerland and Troy McMahon

Give God Some Credit: Risk Taking for the Greater Impact by Brett Andrews

Start a Movement, Plant a Church by Josh Burnett

His Burden is Light: Experiencing Multiplication through Letting Go by K.P. Yohannan

Small Church, Big Impact: A Call for Small Churches to Multiply by Kevin Cox

The Question That Changed My Life: How Planting Life- Giving Churches Became Our Direction by Jeff Leake

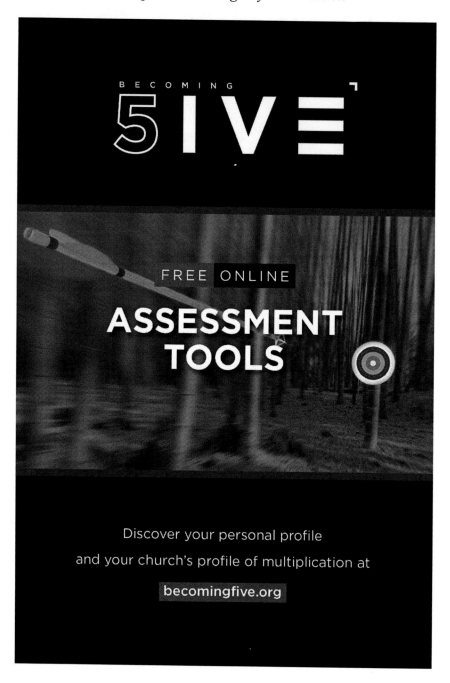

About Todd Wilson

Todd Wilson is co-founder and CEO of Exponential (exponential.org), a community of activists devoted to church multiplication. The international organization's core focus is distributing resources for church multiplication leaders.

Todd received his B.S. in nuclear engineering from North Carolina State University and a master's degree equivalent from the Bettis Atomic Power Laboratory. For 15 years, he served in the Division of Naval Reactors on nuclear submarine design, operation, maintenance, and overhaul.

After a two-year wrestling match with God, Todd entered full-time vocational ministry as the executive pastor at New Life Christian Church where he played a visionary and strategic role for several years as New Life grew and implemented key initiatives such as multisite, externally focused outreach, and church planting. His passion for starting healthy new churches continues to grow. Todd now spends most of his energy engaged in a wide range of leading-edge and pioneering initiatives aimed at helping catalyze movements of healthy, multiplying churches.

Todd has written/co-written multiple books, including *More: Find Your Personal Calling and Live Life to the Fullest Measure* (Zondervan Publishing), *Stories of Sifted* (with Eric Reiss), *Spark: Igniting a Culture of Multiplication, Becoming a Level Five Multiplying Church* (with Dave Ferguson), *Dream Big, Plan Smart: Discover Your Pathway to Level 5 Multiplication* (with Will Mancini), and *Multipliers: Leading Beyond Addition.*

Todd is married to Anna, and they have two sons, Ben and Chris, a beautiful daughter-in-law, Mariah (married to Chris) and another, beautiful, soon to be daughter-in-law, Therese (engaged to Ben).

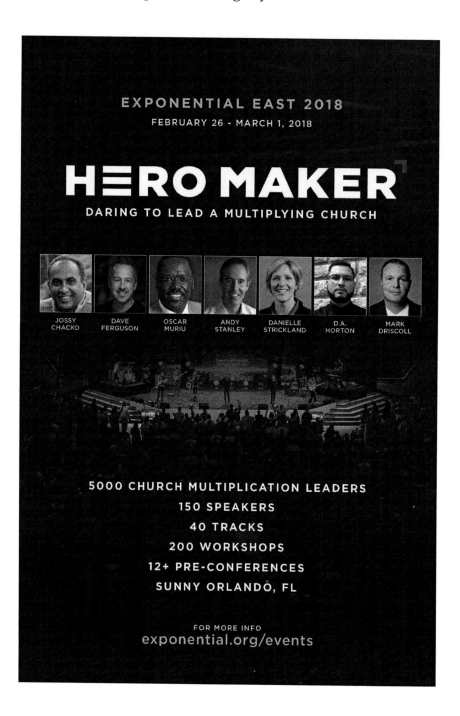

Appendix A
Profiles: Five Levels of Multiplying Churches

Level 1 Profile:

The primary characterizations of Level I churches are "subtraction, scarcity, and survival." Typically, Level 1 churches live with financial tension because they are always worried about having enough money to keep the lights on for Sunday services. They struggle to pay a full-time pastor and then strive toward being able to afford their own facility. As they move to Level 2, most Level 1 churches secure permanent facilities, only exacerbating their financial instability. The continuing financial tensions produce a scarcity mindset that shapes their culture and how they approach ministry.

While the majority of Level 1 churches are small (the average size church in the U.S. runs under 100 attendees), larger churches that have experienced an attendance decline can also be Level 1. The decline produces a financial tension similar to what a smaller church experiences. In a smaller church, the tension is having enough money to pay a full-time pastor and get a building; in a larger church it's having enough money to pay the current staff and a mortgage that may have been secured when more people were giving to the church.

In either case, Level 1 churches operate out of a scarcity mindset. Their planning doesn't look too much beyond getting done what needs to be done for the next couple of weeks. Multiplication doesn't come to mind, and church planting isn't even on the radar. Below are some of the common characteristics of a Level 1 church that you can use to determine where your church is currently:

The senior pastor is running hard to keep up with everything in front of him or her. He is the one that must make all the decisions and hospital visits, officiate weddings and funerals, do the sermon prep, etc. The exhaustive to-do list doesn't leave much time for developing leaders, and he hopes that people are being discipled by his messages. Due to the breadth of the senior minister's responsibilities, the elders are strongly involved in the church's operations. Still, the senior pastor is the one people look to in times of crisis. In fact, in many cases he is the spiritual shepherd, teacher and hero.

The church is dependent on the weekend gatherings for financial viability. So it's not surprising that the weekend services become the focal point for the church. They are designed to satisfy the people that have been attending so the service has a familiar family feel—you usually know who will be there and where they'll be sitting.

In Level 1 churches, most spiritual conversions happen somewhere directly in the presence of the senior pastor or under his or her influence. Because the weekend services (including Sunday school and possibly a prayer service) are the church's primary expression, it isn't difficult to see why people associate "church" with a place or a building.

Churches in this profile typically don't have a systematic plan for developing leaders. While there's talk of growth, most of the energy is spent on keeping up with the needs of people and running Sunday services. Consequently, there's a tendency to lead with "No," and there's not much room for innovation.

Most Level 1 churches would be characterized as consumers rather than producers. Their lack of generosity in releasing people and resources on mission is not due to their lack of compassion and heart. Instead, it's the practical ramification of continually living within a scarcity culture. Leaders live in fear of the future rather than energized by its opportunity.

Most new U.S. church plants are born into Level 1. If they're fortunate to raise enough funds, they may temporarily find themselves in Level 2, but with a countdown clock running as they experience negative cash flow. Most church planters want to be full time with a salary, but that puts significant burden on the new church's finances. Like a business startup, a relatively short window of opportunity exists to either become financially self-sufficient and move into Levels 2 and 3; risk shutting down; or become trapped in a scarcity culture.

Most strategic and vision conversations about the future end with, "we will [fill in the blank] someday when we can afford it." Unfortunately, that elusive day rarely comes for most of the 80 percent of churches in Levels 1 and 2.

The following are a list of characteristics of Level 1 churches. This list is not exhaustive or all-inclusive, and not all Level 1 churches will exhibit all of these characteristics. Don't become overly focused on individual words or characteristics, but instead look at the totality of the culture that the list represents.

- Experiencing decline in some combination of attendance, financial giving, groups/teams, and capacity for maintaining current operations and activities;
- Lack vision and strategy for a future beyond the reality of surviving;
- Scarcity and survival penetrate, inform and shape the culture and decision making;
- Very little conversion growth with most additions through transfers;
- Sense of fear, helplessness and being trapped;
- Often focused on cutting and limiting versus investing and expanding;
- Constrained with bias to "no" rather than "yes";
- Isolated in the community with minimal collaboration in the broader mosaic of organizations impacting their community. Minimal impact or relevance to the community beyond the impact geared to its own members (not externally focused);
- Guarded, protecting and holding on;
- Centralized versus decentralized structure and decision making;

- Most "exercised" leadership is via the senior minister and elders;
- Bias to losing versus attracting staff;
- Small or limited staff and little evidence of the priesthood of all believers being mobilized on mission;
- Shepherding and teaching leadership bias over apostolic and evangelistic impulse;
- Circumstance- versus opportunity-driven;
- Resistant or reluctant to change ("We've never done it that way...");
- Crisis-focused with minimal celebration;
- Tension versus joy and energy;
- Lacking evangelistic zeal;
- Declining budgets and living with the reality of negative cash flow. ("Where should we cut?")
- Loyal core of people carrying out a disproportionate amount of the work;
- Weekend-centric;
- Managing versus leading;
- Unclear, confused, or out-of-alignment vision, mission, values and strategy;
- Bias to the possible versus the impossible;
- Focused on and desiring to stabilize;
- Aging (not necessarily old, but aging congregation with loss or lack of younger people and families);
- Consumed with cutting expenses and how best to add attendance numbers;
- Frequent talk about finances, including the shortfalls

Level 2 Profile:

Level 2 churches have survived and may be growing. They have growth in their sights with Level 3 at the pinnacle, but are constrained by their scarcity thinking. Their focus and aspirations center on growth and addition, and their primary characterizations are "tension, scarcity, survival, and growth."

How do we get to 100? 200? 500? What is our strategy? Do we build? Do we hire a family minister? They are consumed in identifying the actions that will move them toward Level 3. Level 2 churches are often torn by the tyranny of the *or*: "Now that we're financially stable and holding our own, do we put money into staff *or* a permanent facility?" Lacking vision and values for multiplication, the priority of actually releasing resources to multiply just doesn't measure up to the perceived reward at the top of Level 3.

Churches in this profile may be experiencing the "silver bullet syndrome" that causes them to look for that one program or activity or project that will propel them into addition growth.

The lure and appeal of graduating to Level 3 addition is very strong and consumes their thinking.

The following are a list of characteristics of Level 2 churches. This list is not exhaustive or all-inclusive, and not all Level 2 churches will exhibit all of these characteristics. Don't become overly focused on individual words or characteristics, but instead look at the totality of the culture that the list represents:

- Plateaued or possibly stuck. Their scorecard is trending sideways with static attendance, financial giving, etc.;
- Cross-current of tension between survival and growth. Their eyes are fixed on growth (Level 3), but the influence of scarcity thinking at Level 1 constantly pulls on them;
- Experiencing a mixture of characteristics from both Level 1 and Level 3, often being pulled in different directions;
- Living in the tension of, "we will [fill in blank], when we can afford it";
- More susceptible to the "silver bullet" syndrome (i.e., "if we [fill in the blank], we might catalyze growth"). They are continually looking for that important thing that will change their trajectory and put them on the path toward Level 3: Should we add a staff member, a ministry? Do a marketing campaign or outreach event? Or possibly build?

- A stability that allows the church to exhale and catch its breath while trying to figure out the best path forward to Level 3;
- Cautious, reserved, and deliberate. Small steps of risk;
- Tyranny of the OR (we can do this *or* that but not both);
- Overcoming inertia to create momentum;
- Budget-constrained (but at least not having to cut like Level 1).
- Afraid/fearful of losing people.
- Susceptible to making decisions to preserve, please and keep people happy rather than being bold to seize new opportunities;
- No (or minimal) leadership development pipeline;
- Multiplication/church planting is a distant future hope versus a current reality as it competes with limited resources within their OR mentality;
- Emerging hope and optimism (if they're moving forward from Level 1) OR increasing fear and uncertainty (if they're declining backward from Level 3). Tension, uncertainty and fog about the future. These churches are looking for a clear picture toward Level 3;
- Leveraging gifting of staff and elders versus releasing the capacity of the church;
- Lacking clarity or strong conviction to act in alignment with vision, mission, values and strategy;
- Focusing on strategies for adding numbers consumes more time than focusing on biblical disciple making. Instinctively, the pathway to Level 3 is implementing strategies that add attendance;
- May be in the process of refining their governance and core processes to move from centralized to more decentralized approaches, with a number of simultaneous, subtle transitions happening;
- Often focused on "how do we [fill in the blank]?"
- Fearful of instability or decline;
- Church-centric. It's difficult to look beyond managing inside the church;
- Vision and strategy are unifying, but often with focus on the macro-addition strategies of Level 3

Level 3 Profile:

Level 3 churches have shown success at growth. Their leaders are conquerors with a demonstrated record of taking the next hill. The primary characterizations of these churches are "addition, growth and accumulation."

These churches have grown accustomed to finding and solving the problems that limit growth. They've dealt with rapid year-over-year growth in budgets; building and facility decisions; capital campaigns and assuming debt; building teams; staffing (including hiring and firing); structural issues (including infrastructure and overhead); the drive for the next innovative marketing and outreach strategies; and reorganizations to improve organizational alignment.

Level 3 churches live and breathe macro-addition. They are opportunity-oriented with a bias to "where or what is the next one?" They and their peers have inherited the addition-growth scorecard of their spiritual fathers and are products of the church growth movement of the past 30 years.

Churches in this profile don't *want* to fundamentally be about the numbers, but they also know that numbers matter. Income is directly proportional to attendance, and the number of volunteers needed increases as attendance numbers increase.

These churches experience a constant tension and delicate symbiotic balance between increasing attendance numbers; increasing financial giving numbers; and increasing volunteer hours. Out of necessity, staff often function as managers and coordinators rather than disciple makers. Thus, the constant tension between making biblical disciples and cultural Christians is always lurking. The time, energy, and effort needed to model biblical disciple making from the top down and the bottom up simply doesn't fit the demands of a rapid numerical growth culture. As a result, the focus shifts to "leadership development systems" rather than biblical disciple making. In case you're wondering, here's the difference between the two. *Leadership development* is more systematic and impersonal, focusing on developing skills and competencies, whereas *biblical disciple making* takes time and effort at the relational level and focuses on character, surrender, calling, and obedience.

These leadership development systems are essential to building capacity at the local level (our definition of macro-addition activities). In most cases, these systems center on the goal of supporting internal growth in the local church versus creating a source of leaders to *go*.

For these Level 3 churches, releasing resources to macro-multiplication directly competes with the very resources that fuel their macro-addition strategies. And only one wins out!

Leaders of Level 3 churches are at a crucial point in their development in terms of setting the course of their future: addition-growth culture versus multiplication-growth culture. Their choices are numerous "line in the sand" decisions that could potentially shape their core values, convictions and practices. The path for most of the churches in this profile keeps them captive and stuck, unable to move beyond Level 3 multiplication.

The following is a list of characteristics of Level 3 churches. This list is not exhaustive or all-inclusive, and not all Level 3 churches will exhibit all of these characteristics. Don't become overly focused on individual words or characteristics, but instead look at the totality of the culture that the list represents:

- Dollar-dependent versus disciple-dependent;
- Resource allocation (e.g., staff, facilities, programs) is often in support of increased "butts in seats" (attendance);
- Local capacity building is far more focused on producing and maintaining addition-growth than on making, developing and deploying biblical disciples;
- Accumulation and numerical growth;

- "Customer orientation": who is the customer, what do they value and how do we deliver that value?
- Can unintentionally mistake or overvalue participation over transformation;
- "Growth strategies" and growth seasons are never ending. Staff is often challenged with "What will we do to grow in this upcoming opportunity season?";
- Opportunity-biased ... for numerical growth;
- Adding local capacity to grow numbers. Most resources (financial and people) are put into local church growth with minimal allocated to Kingdom capacity via new churches;
- Focused on growing the church versus changing the community or city;
- Constant tension between adding cultural Christians who need to be fed AND making biblical disciples who mature to be sent;
- Leading *and* managing;
- These churches are learning to leverage the "genius of the AND" for growth, but not so much for multiplication;
- Allocating resources: staff, buildings, programs, outreach, marketing, etc.;
- Decentralized structure and control with increased emphasis on groups and teams;
- "Multi" thinking: multisite, multicultural, multi-service style, etc. Focused on increasing the "flavors" and "options" rather than preserving the past;
- Innovative risk-taking when it comes to addition-growth strategies;
- Debt;
- Program- and event-driven with major emphasis on Sunday services;
- Conquerors. Overcoming next barriers, obstacles and hills. Continually progressing through the next series of "false" summits to find the next one waiting;
- Staff led;
- Early adopters (and often pioneers) in the diffusion of innovation theory;

- Competitive and driven with an eye toward being on the various largest and fastest-growing churches lists;
- Opportunistic (seeing the opportunity and seizing it), especially for increased growth. Learning to discern between great and good opportunities;
- Evangelistic impulse via large group preaching and events is often stronger than the relational work of biblical disciple making (producing disciples who make disciples). Strategies at Level 3 are often characterized by churches making disciples rather than disciples making disciples;
- Often higher concentration of apostolic and evangelistic leadership;
- Excitement, energy and momentum;
- Frequent celebration, story and inspiration;
- "We can do it, you can help" versus "You can do it, we can help" approach;
- Significant resources required to "feed the beast" and run the church compared with resources allocated to developing and sending people to start new churches;
- Often values excellence;
- Scorecard: Attendance ("butts in seats"), financial giving and decisions (baptisms). Spiritual formation is often not given the same weight;
- Increasing complexity is difficult to reproduce;
- Holy discontent of senior leader may emerge ("There must be something more than simply growing things bigger.");
- The things birthed outside the walls of the church are typically connected to growth inside the church;
- Churchwide campaigns of various shapes and sizes;
- Family-friendly (e.g., often a strong children's and youth focus);
- Solid leadership development systems emerge, but often to fuel the increased required local capacity needed in the local church (rather than for sending leaders to start new churches)

Level 4 Profile:

The primary characterizations for Level 4 churches include "discontent, new scorecards, and reproducing at all levels." Leaders of these churches sense that there is something more than conquering addition-growth and are drawn to a future that's more about planting new orchards than putting more trees in their orchard.

Level 4 leaders also sense something new and fresh. Maybe they've already embraced a different scorecard, or maybe they're simply feeling a holy discontent that something needs to change. They almost instinctively know that "more of the same will not get us to where we need to go." They desire and are willing to move to Level 5, and might be making progress, but the tensions and force pulling them back to Level 3 limits their ability to move more fully into Level 5.

Level 4 churches demonstrate the ability to reproduce leaders, services, and sites/campuses. But their discontent pulls them toward different motives for reproducing. Their reasons for reproduction become more about macro-multiplication to build Kingdom capacity than macro-addition to build local church capacity.

These churches are as passionate about leadership development systems that intentionally produce leaders to *go* as they are about systems that develop leaders to stay. They are birthing and taking ownership of a strong value of multiplication, including putting behaviors and practices in place that are consistent with Level 5 churches.

Level 4 churches live in tension. They are torn between a vision for multiplication at Level 5 and the reality of the demands created by Level 3 macro-addition practices. The resources needed to deploy and send for multiplication are typically the best resources for fueling Level 3 growth.

The following is a list of characteristics of Level 4 churches. This list is not exhaustive or all-inclusive, and not all Level 4 churches will exhibit all of these characteristics. Don't become overly focused on individual words or characteristics, but instead look at the totality of the culture that the list represents:

- Experiencing strong tension between the demands of macro-addition and the desire for macro-multiplication. These churches want more multiplication but feel constrained by the demands of maintaining the overhead required for the macro-addition strategies they have in place;
- Experiencing reproduction at various levels including multisite and church planting;
- Decision-making and resource allocation are still strongly influenced by Level 3 macro-addition, but these churches also have a demonstrated commitment to multiplication. They allocate resources to specific multiplication practices such as leadership internships/residencies, support services for church planters, participation in and affiliation with church planting networks or associations, and direct funding of church planting;
- Reproducing happens through discipline, intentionality, and a multiplication strategy;
- These churches are often more aggressive with their multisite strategy than their church planting strategy;
- Sacrificial and generous, contributing their first fruits of leaders and money to church multiplication;
- Scorecard that includes macro-multiplication activities such as number of churches planted, number of church planters trained, percent of income allocated to church planting, and number of leaders deployed;
- These churches are as passionate about releasing and sending as they are about accumulating and growing;
- Value is placed on leadership development that leads to reproducing and multiplying churches;
- Multiplication may still be more activity-based than values-based, and may not transcend beyond the tenure of the senior pastor;

- Multiplication is typically more deliberate and planned than it is spontaneous, and often occurs with staff and interns. These churches are starting to see lay people being called and mobilized to "go" and be part of church planting;
- These churches regularly celebrate and highlight the impact of the churches they start, using the opportunity to inspire others to be involved;
- People in the church see church planting as a Kingdom-focused activity of the church that requires sacrifice;
- Leadership development pipeline is healthy and active, fueling the Level 3 activities of the church as well as church multiplication.
- Micro-multiplication is a key element of adding disciples. Biblical disciple making is strong, with disciples making disciples who make disciples. The natural fruit of this strong disciple-making culture is a pool of leaders willing to *go* and be part of starting new churches;
- People in the church are regularly called to join and be part of church planting teams, including the sacrifice to move;
- Because of their reputation, Level 4 churches tend to attract leaders from outside the church who are interested in church planting;
- Tend to start local church planting networks or affiliate with existing ones;
- Often have a full- or part-time staff person overseeing their church planting activities;
- Senior leaders have a natural "holy discontent" that causes a bias for action toward Level 5 behaviors;
- Exhibit significant financial commitment to church planting;
- Releasing staff is more intentional in Level 4 compared with Level 3 where it is often reactive;
- Collaborative, teachable bias with Kingdom perspective;
- Heart for the lost;
- Competition is no longer other churches, but instead the obstacles to increased multiplication;
- *Go* culture and bias

Level 5 Profile:

Level 5 churches are rare, so they stick out in the crowd. The primary characterizations for these churches are "multiplying, releasing, and sending." Their leaders spend as much time on macro-multiplication strategies and activities as they do on macro-addition.

Churches in this profile will plant hundreds of churches and send thousands of people to be part of church planting teams over their lifespan. Their scorecard is more about "who has been sent" than "how many have been accumulated." They demonstrate many of the same characteristics of Level 3 and 4 churches, but are distinguished by behaviors:

- Level 5 churches have church planting interns/residents in training who will be sent to launch new churches within the next 12 months.

- They are more focused on multiplying new churches than they are on growing their own church larger and conquering the next attendance barrier.

- They contribute substantial financial resources (at least 10 percent) from the first fruits of their budget to church planting. They are continually looking for ways to increase and leverage the amount. They also tithe (at least) to church planting on any funds raised for buildings and mortgage debt.

- They choose to plant their first autonomous church before assuming land and building debt.

- They decide to plant their first autonomous church before launching their own first campus or multisite.

- They have a specific plan for doubling their church planting activity—not a dream or vision, but rather a specific plan for guiding and making it happen.

- They release and send out their first church planter before accumulating several staff members, and then they continue to send staff, releasing the first fruits of their leadership capacity in a regular and ongoing way.

- They publicly and regularly call their members to *go* and be part of church planting teams.

- They regularly celebrate their church planting activities in a way that inspires others to get involved. They celebrate in a way that helps people see how they can be involved versus simply hearing about what others are doing.

- They publicly and regularly call their members to give sacrificially above and beyond their tithe to the local church to support church planting and specific church plants.

- They are actively affiliated with and participating in a church planting network (or denominational initiative) that's committed to multiplication. Often, they are the founding members of these networks.

Churches that consistently practice and exhibit these behaviors close the gap between aspirations and reality. The persistent focus and sacrifice toward macro-multiplication creates a culture of multiplication in these churches. These Level 5 churches develop a DNA so strongly centered on multiplication that they would have to *try* not to multiply.

The following is a list of characteristics of Level 5 churches. This list is not exhaustive or all-inclusive, and not all Level 5 churches will exhibit all of these characteristics. Don't become overly focused on individual words or characteristics, but instead look at that totality of the culture that the list represents:

- These churches would have to *try* not to multiply. Multiplication is deeply embedded in their DNA;

- Multiplication seems to happen spontaneously and is not limited to paid staff;
- Mobilize the priesthood of all believers;
- Biblical disciple making is strong, with much of the church's growth occurring as disciples make disciples who make disciples;
- Strategies are simple and reproducible;
- Have a different scorecard rooted in sending and releasing capacity versus adding and accumulating;
- Solid balance of the Ephesians five-fold gifting and with a strong apostolic impulse;
- Aggressive intern and residency program (leadership development pipeline leading to church plants);
- Focused on pastoring and transforming a city/geographic area versus building and growing a church;
- Significant commitment of financial resources to macro-multiplication (e.g., >10+ of tithes and offerings);
- Routinely releasing staff AND members to planting;
- Every disciple is a potential church planter/team member;
- Daughter church plants carry the DNA and are also active in church planting/sending;
- Decision making and resource allocation is always through the lens of church multiplication;
- Activities and commitment transcend the tenure of the senior pastor;
- Marketplace/lay leaders are routinely released/sent to plant churches;
- Regular and ongoing celebration of multiplication stories and impact;
- Regularly call members to sacrifice financially in giving to church planting. These churches are as inclined to run church-planting campaigns as they are church-building campaigns;
- Have systems to develop, deploy and support church-planting leaders and teams;
- Regularly coach and help leaders outside the church who are planting churches;

- Often part of (or founding members in) a church planting network or association;
- Develop best practices for others to follow;
- Solid balance between macro-addition and macro-multiplication;
- Abundance mentality with a big vision and goals for impact beyond the walls of the church;
- "Spiritual fathers" to children, grandchildren, and great grandchild churches;
- Movement mentality

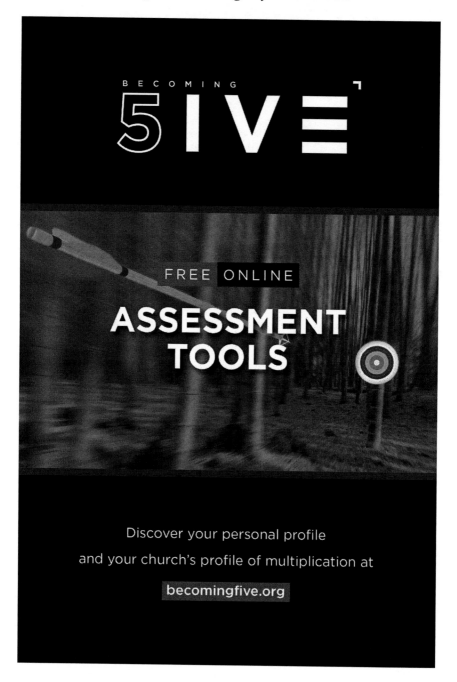

Appendix B
Pathways to Multiplication

Based on your results from the Becoming 5 online assessment, what is your pathway to multiplication? The last two numbers of your multiplication pattern indicate your specific pathway. Use the following descriptions to better understand the journey to multiplication for your pathway. You may want to leverage this clarity to refine and adjust your multiplication vision.

Level 3 to 4

Level 3 characteristics: Level 3 churches make up approximately 16 percent of all U.S. churches. For these churches, the scorecard is rooted in addition growth and accumulation. Level 3 churches build their budgets around key growth drivers, including buildings, staff, programs, outreach, marketing, etc. They find it difficult to release and send out their best staff and volunteers to plant churches.

These churches tend to be programmatic with centralized control and decision-making processes. They know how to add (or reproduce) worship services and may have reproduced sites or locations as part of their growth strategy. They have a history of conquering the next growth barrier. As they consider moving to Level 4, these churches often feel *significant* tensions holding them back. Reallocating their time, talent and treasure for multiplication is painful because the resources necessary for church planting compete with the resources needed to fuel the addition-growth activities they've become addicted to.

Often, Level 3 churches are strong at corporate evangelistic activities and programmatic growth but weak on biblical disciple making. They tend to add disciples primarily through corporate, programmatic means rather than through relational discipleship, with disciples making disciples.
As we discussed in chapter 3, these churches have a strong bias to building addition capacity vs. building multiplication capacity.

Addition capacity becomes the primary means for adding disciples. Level 3 churches are strong at mobilizing volunteers for church service, but weaker on mobilizing disciples as 24/7 missionaries into every corner of society. For them, volunteer mobilization is vital to feeding the addition capacity-centered activities that fuel addition growth, with virtually no emphasis on mobilizing people in their uniqueness and calling for purposes outside the church.

Tensions: The tensions that hold these churches back from Level 4 are rooted in an operating system and DNA that optimizes addition activities to the exclusion of multiplication. Addition-focused operating systems are so deeply embedded in these churches that it would be difficult (if not impossible) to create the level of change necessary for Level 5 multiplication without overhauling the church. For this reason, a more reasonable first step for a Level 3 church is to aspire to and move to Level 4.

From 3 to 4: The move to Level 4 plays to the strength of a Level 3 church. This shift is programmatic and does not require deeply rooted change. Level 3 churches can actually program their way to Level 4. They simply need to embrace the journey to Level 4 with the same diligence and commitment as conquering the next growth hill. If your pathway is 3-4, you'll need to:

- Adjust your scorecard to include multiplication dimensions.
- Embrace multiplication beyond local multisite expressions.
- Treat church planting/multiplication with the same intensity as any other major new initiative or priority.
- Reallocate financial resources to multiplication.
- Set goals for church planting.
- Consider raising up and releasing leaders to plant churches, including encouraging staff to think about planting.
- Join a church-planting network, engage via their denomination, and/or affiliate with other churches that seek to plant churches.

The most direct path to Level 4 is churches themselves practicing the principle of first fruits, giving the first 10 percent of their income to church planting; encouraging their best staff and volunteers to leave and plant churches; and committing valuable time and leadership capacity to direct involvement in church planting.

To get to Level 4, Level 3 churches must shift and reallocate some of their programming resources to church planting and multiplication.

Level 4 to 4+

Level 4 characteristics: Level 4 churches make up approximately 4 percent of all U.S. churches. These churches have already made the programmatic shift to allocate their time, talent and treasure to church planting and multiplication. At a minimum they invest financially, often at least 10 percent of their tithes and offerings to church planting. These churches are committed to church planting and tend to press for increased involvement among the laity.

Tensions: Level 4 churches continually live in the tension of wanting to increase their church-planting activities but feeling the strain of resourcing their local church operations and growth. These churches recognize the importance of biblical disciple making and that the natural fruit of a strong disciple-making culture is a pool of leaders willing to go and be part of starting new churches. However, like Level 3 churches, they still struggle with weak disciple-making systems. The lack of strong biblical disciple making is a distinct tension holding back Level 4 churches from Level 5 multiplication.

From 4 to 4+: Although the shift from Level 4 to 4+ often happens naturally over time, Level 4 churches can expedite this shift by being strategic and intentional. Churches moving from 4 to 4+ always have a vision larger than growing their local church. They see their church through a Kingdom lens rather than seeing the Kingdom through the lens of their local church.

At the heart of transformation of Summit Church in Raleigh, North Carolina, from addition to multiplication is the idea of sending, says Planter/Pastor J.D. Greear:

"We've grown to be the sort of culture where sending is in the very air we breathe. Being a disciple means being sent; so sending should pervade *every* aspect of what a church does. First-time guests should know from the moment they set foot on our campuses that sending and Kingdom are in our blood."[4] Churches moving from Level 4 to 4+ typically demonstrate an increasing number of the following types of behaviors:

- Reproduction happens through discipline, intentionality, and a multiplication strategy.
- Reproduction occurs at various levels, including multisite and church planting. However, these churches are more aggressive with their church-planting strategy than their multisite strategy.
- Their scorecard includes multiplication activities such as the number of churches planted; number of church planters trained; percentage of income allocated to church planting; and number of leaders deployed.
- They regularly multiplication wins, highlighting the impact of the churches they start and leveraging the opportunity to inspire others to be involved.
- They give sacrificially to multiplication, contributing their first fruits (both money and leadership)—typically at least 10 percent of their tithes and offerings.
- Decision-making and resource allocation are still strongly influenced by Level 3 demands. But these churches also have a demonstrated commitment to multiplication. They allocate resources to specific multiplication practices such as leadership internships/residencies; support services for church planters; participation in and affiliation with church-planting networks or associations; and direct funding of church planting.
- A healthy and active leadership development pipeline fuels the Level 3 activities of the church, as well as church multiplication.

- Releasing staff is more intentional compared with Level 3, where it is often reactive. In moving to 4+, releasing key staff becomes more intentional and frequent.
- Multiplication is typically more deliberate and planned than it is spontaneous, and often occurs with staff and interns. These churches are just starting to see lay people respond to God's call to "go" and be part of church planting.
- They are as passionate about releasing and sending as they are about accumulating and growing.
- The congregation sees church planting as a Kingdom-focused activity of the church that requires sacrifice.
- They have a bias to "go"—with a high value of mobilizing people in their area of giftedness and calling.
- Leaders regularly call church members to join and be part of church-planting teams, including the sacrifice to move to a new city or state.
- Senior leaders have a natural "holy discontent"—often resulting in a bias toward Level 5 behaviors.
- They've hired a full- or part-time staff person to oversee their church-planting activities.
- Their reputation for church planting is growing, attracting outside leaders who are interested in church planting.
- They tend to start local church-planting networks or affiliate with existing ones.
- Competition is no longer other churches, but instead the obstacles to increased multiplication.

New to 4

New church characteristics: Most new churches define their success using the prevailing Level 3 scorecard. They launch at Level 2 or 3 and spend several years struggling to become financially self-sufficient. Church planters tend to focus on the perceived stability of a Level 3 church, significantly influenced by the prevailing belief that at Level 3, a church is "successful." The various church lists (Fastest Growing, Largest, Most Innovative, etc.) are powerful shaping factors for new church planters. The average church plant does not have a vision for Level 4 or 5 multiplication. Instead, they embrace the "someday" philosophy: "Someday, when we can afford it, we will get involved in church planting." Unfortunately, for most churches that elusive day never comes.

During their first five years, most churches struggle financially, often bouncing between Level 1, 2 and 3, and always uncertain about their future. Most remain at Levels 1 or 2 (with many closing their doors) while some emerge at Level 3.

Tensions: For churches seeking to launch at Level 4, financial stresses are the top barrier. Their commitment to the principle of investing their first fruits in church planting uniquely distinguishes them from 99 percent of all church plants.

From New to 4: New church planters seeking to launch at Level 4 embrace that vision during their church's pre-launch. They commit to implementing as many Level 4 behaviors and values into their DNA as possible—making tough, risky decisions that buck prevailing wisdom. They know that the behaviors and decisions they make during the launch phase will ultimately shape and direct their future. They step out on faith to invest financially before it makes sense or before they can afford it. From the start, they commit the first fruits of their time, talent and treasure to church planting; get involved with a network/denomination to immediately help plant other churches; and they seek church-planting residents/interns who will go and plant churches within the first few years of their launch. Churches in this pathway plant pregnant. They commit to the following types of behaviors:

- Tithing to church planting.
- Launching pregnant with a church-planting intern or resident in place.
- Planting their first church before launching their first multisite.
- Planting their first church within the first three years after launch.
- Planting their first church before buying land or taking on mortgage debt.

- Setting goals for church planting during their first three, five and 10 years.
- Joining or affiliating with a church-planting network or denomination.
- Prioritizing church planting, building it into their bylaws and founding documents.
- Seeking to hire staff with the potential to plant churches.

The concept of "planting pregnant" became a reality for Revolution Annapolis planters Josh and Sarah Burnett. As they began to work on their staffing plan for the church they would plant, the only non-negotiable was a church planter in residence. Two years into launching Revolution, the church sent out their church planters in residence, Scott and Amber Nancaro, to plant The Foundry in Baltimore, Maryland.

Burnett shares his story in the free eBook *Plant Pregnant: Leaving a Legacy of Disciples.* "If we're going to actually see a movement of church planting happen in America, then church plants will have to step up and plant pregnant. And the churches they plant will need to have the same DNA and conviction to plant pregnant.[5]

Like Level 3 churches that move to Level 4 or 4+, these new churches can move to Level 4 programmatically and without strong biblical disciple-making systems in place. However, unless they build into their DNA a balanced approach to the three dimensions of multiplication (disciple making, capacity building, and empowering mobilization), moving to Level 5 is an almost impossible feat.

New to 5

As I've said before, Level 5 multiplication requires a new operating system and wineskin. Because they don't have to overcome the resistance of changing existing DNA, new churches offer the greatest potential for creating new Level 5 expressions of the future. They have the freedom and flexibility to try new approaches.

Level 5 churches dream big and expect God-sized results.

Tensions: The greatest challenge here is the lack of models and examples in the U.S. church to learn from and emulate. That's why I turned to Ralph Moore, who leads one of the few Level 5 church movements (Hope Chapel) in the United States, to learn about the factors vital for launching at Level 5. Moore says new churches must:

- Build into their DNA simple, reproducible systems and processes that are accessible to the average Christian.
- Make disciple makers. More than 90 percent of Level 5 multiplication is solid, biblical disciple making, Moore says, because the fruit of healthy disciple making is multiplication.
- Create a scorecard that values and celebrates multiplication.
- Focus on a leadership development pipeline that releases and sends out leaders, producing multiplication via new churches rather than simply fueling local growth.
- Instill a Kingdom perspective with big goals rather than local church perspective limited to local goals.
- Champion a strong bias to bi-vocational marketplace pastors.
- Start with and continue to raise up humble, yet tenacious, Level 5 leaders who can and will surrender their own egos.
- Live with an urgency and conviction that hell is real, and that those around us are dying spiritual deaths.

Additionally, below is a list of Level 5 characteristics Dave Ferguson and I presented in *Becoming a Level Five Multiplying Church*:

- Level 5 churches would have to *try* not to multiply. Multiplication is deeply embedded in their DNA.
- Multiplication seems to happen spontaneously and isn't limited to paid staff.
- Level 5 churches mobilize the priesthood of all believers to live deployed lives as 24/7 missionaries in their individual, unique corners of society.

- Biblical disciple making is strong, with much of the church's growth occurring as disciples making disciples who make disciples.
- Strategies are simple and reproducible.
- They have a different scorecard rooted in sending and releasing capacity vs. adding and accumulating.
- They have a solid balance of the fivefold gifting (Ephesians 4) with a strong apostolic impulse.
- They develop an aggressive intern and residency program (leadership development pipeline leading to church plants).
- They focus on pastoring and transforming a city/geographic area versus building and growing a church.
- They allocate significant financial resources to macro-multiplication (e.g., greater than 10 percent of their tithes and offerings).
- They routinely release staff and members to planting.
- Every disciple is a potential church planter/team member.
- Daughter church plants carry the multiplication DNA and are also active in church planting/sending.
- Decision-making and resource allocation always happen through the lens of church multiplication.
- Multiplication activities and commitment transcend the tenure of the senior pastor.
- They routinely release and send marketplace/lay leaders to plant churches.
- They regularly tell and celebrate stories of multiplication and impact.
- They regularly call members to sacrifice financially to church planting and are as inclined to run church-planting campaigns as they are church-building campaigns.
- They create and sustain systems to develop, deploy and support church-planting leaders and teams.
- They regularly coach and help leaders outside the church who are planting churches.
- Leaders are often founding members or part of a church-planting network or association.
- They develop best practices for others to follow.

- They strike a solid balance between addition-capacity building and multiplication-capacity building;
- They have an abundance mentality with a big vision for impact beyond the walls of the church.
- They are "spiritual fathers" to children, grandchildren, and great grandchild churches.
- They lead with a "movement" mentality.[6]

Additionally, Level 5 multiplication integrates the three dimensions of multiplication, the 10 characteristics of Level 5 churches, and the five shifts required for Level 5 multiplication. To see a Level 5 movement of multiplication like Moore's Hope Chapel, we must include all of these factors into our vision and plan. Ralph Moore is collaborating with SEND Network Vice President Jeff Christopherson (members of our Becoming Five team) on an eBook focusing on the "New to 5" pathway. Look for this new resource in early 2017.

Level 1 or 2 to 4

Level 1 and 2 churches live in a scarcity culture underneath continuous stress, causing them to focus on Level 3 as the solution. In some ways, the Level 1 or 2 church experiences many of the same dynamics as those in the "New to 4" pathway. However, the new church often has external funding for several years.

These churches have three pathways to Level 4:

- First, like a new church, Level 1 or 2 churches can faithfully commit to investing the first fruits of their time, talent and treasure into church planting and multiplication. Just as we teach our members to tithe regardless of their financial situation, churches should do the same. However, their scarcity culture and financial reality make this commitment difficult. It is a very tough pathway, but the key question for Level 1 and 2 churches aspiring to Level 4 is, "Will you put Level 4 behaviors in place even when the financial and human resource balance sheets suggest it's impossible?" One prudent path is to take the list of Level 4 behaviors and simply "downsize" it to smaller steps and/or choose a few items to focus on and pursue.

- Second, a church could follow conventional wisdom and wait until they can afford it. Of course, the biblical foundation for this path is weak, and the elusive day of investing in church planting rarely ever comes when taking this pathway.

- The third option is to focus on getting to Level 3 in a way that can springboard the church to Level 4 using the "3- 4" core pathway (described above). Churches that follow this path must understand and grasp the reality that many of the strategies for getting to Level 3 create roadblocks to moving on to Level 4. If you're serious about Level 4 and take this path through Level 3, be cautious in embracing Level 3 behaviors that actually hinder Level 4 progress.

Levels 1, 2, 3, or 4 to 5

For most churches, the new operating system that Level 5 requires will only be possible by shutting down for three to six months and relaunching, using the "New to 5" pathway. Practically, we know that this means most existing churches will focus on moving to Level 4 (or 4+) rather than Level 5.

However, Level 3 and 4 churches do have the resource base for experimenting and piloting new expressions that may help create new pathways for existing churches moving to Level 5. For now, we have yet to discover the pathway needed to move existing churches to Level 5.

exponential.org

Appendix C
Tensions of Multiplication

In *Spark: Igniting a Culture of Multiplication,* we highlighted 18 different tensions that leaders will face in moving from Levels 1, 2, and 3 to Levels 4 and 5. Level 4 multiplier Larry Walkemeyer first introduced these tensions in his book, *Flow: Unleashing a River of Multiplication in Your Church, City and World.* Following is the full list:

Tension #1: Here or There (Addition or Multiplication)
Should we focus on growing our attendance, or starting new places of growth?

In many ways, the most obvious metric for success for churches has been the number of people in attendance. Larger attendance numbers mean a bigger platform, which means more resources, perceived flexibility and perceived influence. Addition-growth leaders prioritize their church's energy, money, talent, volunteers and leaders to help grow attendance. The primary lens of decision-making centers on building bigger and bigger churches. We need a "here *and* there" approach.

Walkemeyer suggests relearning "Kingdom math" to guide this shift: "Addition is adept at bringing glory to God and to us; multiplication requires humility lived out. Multiplication demonstrates an 'it's not about us' dimension to ministry. It builds a different scoreboard—one that lights up when new leaders are sent out instead of simply when new consumers come in. The glory of the local church gets lost in the glory of the Kingdom."

While the number of people attending weekend services is a valid metric, building a culture of multiplication means talking about success differently. Fortunately, we don't have to choose one option over the other. The Church is designed to deliver both. We simply need to cooperate in that design.

215

Tension #2: Facility Acquisition vs. Facility Sacrifice
Should we focus on a church building that will establish us in the community, or invest those resources in planting?

Apart from the metric of attendance, people often look to structures as an important measurement of success. Often, when people talk about "church," they're referencing buildings and structures rather than the people who make up that church community. Again, there is great temptation to fall for this simple rule of thumb: A bigger church facility is directly proportional to greater success. We've bought into the 1980s film *Field of Dreams* message–"If you build it, they will come."

Leaders that build on actual values of planting and multiplication will sacrifice—willingly and joyfully—some of their comfort (for example, a permanent church facility, new carpet or air conditioning, the latest technical gear, etc.) for the sake of multiplying the Kingdom. This kind of atypical sacrifice can be jarring in our consumer culture. However, we believe that embracing this countercultural value will help point your church toward radical multiplication.

A decision to build or buy a building, or add to an existing one, before planting your first church may lock you into an addition-growth culture that becomes increasingly more difficult to overcome.

Tension #3: Financial Security vs. Financial Uncertainty
Should we prioritize our financial stability or, in an act of faith, commit our financial resources to planting?

Jesus tells us in Luke 14 that His disciples will need to count the cost of following Him. For aspiring Level 5 multipliers, very real costs and risks are involved—particularly in a financial sense. As the idea of multiplication takes root in your church's imagination and value systems, you'll need to be prepared not only to love the idea but also navigate these financial tensions.

People will naturally want to know the return on investment in planting new churches. Staff and other leaders will wonder how prioritizing your church's financial resources toward multiplication will impact their current ministries. It will be easy for many of your leaders to show that investing the resources into existing ministries or starting new sites is better stewardship. Still, others might suggest reaching specific financial goals before committing resources to planting. Without a strong core conviction to multiply, you *will* succumb to the addition-growth culture pathways.

Drawing from leadership consultant Brian Zehr's experience, many churches want to move to radical or exponential multiplication, but hit a roadblock when they realize the cost involved. Sometimes, even gathering leaders and resources for new ministries only further entrenches a culture of addition if the actual culture isn't changing toward multiplication.

Walkemeyer reminds us: "The reality is God is bigger than the *X*. God is not limited to our savings account. Jesus taught us to lay up our treasures above, not on earth. He wasn't denigrating savings accounts, but He was establishing priorities. Our security is not in more *X* number of dollars but in the ability of God and in His promises to those who follow His Kingdom priorities. We can trust the Almighty or the Dollar, but not both."

Tension #4: Attractional vs. 'Activational'
Should we try to draw more people by offering more comfort and better programs? Or challenge them to live sacrificially on mission with God?

"Have it your way" is more than a slogan for a fast food chain; it's a way of life in our consumer culture. In the push to grow ever-larger churches, addition culture can overemphasize the needs and desires of potential church members. Most often, the churches that grow the most provide the highest-quality religious goods and services.

However, that attractional impulse to draw in and retain is directly opposite to creating a culture of releasing, sending and multiplication. Attractional priorities in church ministry look for activities that reinforce attachment to the local church. Conversely, "activational" priorities challenge believers to do what is difficult—to avoid growing too attached to the amenities of the mother church but instead seek ways to engage in the mission of multiplication.

Our temptation is to cater to the consumers who will fund their own comfort instead of calling out the missionaries who will commit to building the Kingdom. The reality is that most churches are planted into survival (subtraction) culture, simply trying to build up enough members and resources to become self-sustaining. The desperation of survival in those early days can lead to a strong impulse in the attractional activities that fuel addition growth. Those early days of building culture are naturally drawn to addition-growth paradigms, and these roots become increasingly difficult to pull up as the church gets older.

Tension #5: Filling Our Church vs. Starting A New Church
Should we focus on reaching a certain attendance goal before starting a new church, or begin planting regardless?

If you champion radical multiplication, make no mistake, you *will* face the tension of having empty space in the mother church that needs to be filled before considering starting a new church. You'll likely hear: "Why start something new when what we have is not full? Why not focus energy on this objective instead of dissipating energy by launching a new church?" Until the seats are full at multiple services at the mother church, there will be great temptation to delay planting.

The reality, though, is that there is no perfect set of conditions (attendance, finances, staffing, etc.) that will guarantee success for either the mother church or the plant. To move toward a radical multiplication culture, you'll need to recognize the remnant of addition culture that thinks attendance growth is the foundational key to success in planting.

Tension #6: New Campus vs. New Plant
Should we start a multisite campus, or plant a new church?

Facing this tension requires some soul searching and hard questions about what model of multisite you plan to implement, as well as your ultimate goal in starting a new campus. If the new campus is, in reality, simply overflow rooms that further showcase or deploy your gifts, then know you're likely acting from an addition-growth paradigm.

However, if your church is considering a new multisite location as a means to leverage the strength of the mother church whose goals include raising up new teaching; developing new indigenous leadership; creating new vision that addresses location-specific needs; *and* eventually starting a site or plant itself, then your church may be bucking the norm and innovating an approach that is more characteristic of multiplication.

Be aware that the energy you and your church expend to start and maintain a multisite campus can quickly drain the energy and resources for multiplying new churches. Multisite strategy can easily inhibit true multiplication, but it also can be an accelerator of it.

Is each new site positioned, equipped and expected to reproduce into additional new sites from their context in the same way the mother or original campus does with its new sites? In other words, is each new site simply just new services created to extend the reach of the mother campus? Or is each new site expected to replicate additional sites the way the mother campus does?

Tension #7: Senior Leader Coasting vs. Senior Leader Climbing
Should I build systems that allow me to coast, or continue to ride uphill?

Navigating this tension requires you to honestly assess your personal energy and resiliency. Church planting can feel like riding a bicycle uphill. Then, just when you're about to crest the hill and coast for a season, you choose to turn right and start up a new hill. Most leaders find themselves focused on leveraging their energy to build a system, allowing them then to decrease their energy investment as they and their organization mature. Few leaders want to keep making multiplication choices that require increased leadership energy. Leaders who grasp the Kingdom value of building multiplication cultures in their churches rise up to meet these uphill challenges.

Tension #8: Staffing the Mother Church vs. Staffing the Plants
Should we hang on to our best staff members, or send them out as church planters?

Leadership development is a significant and difficult task, in and of itself. But to then take the step of sending out those flourishing leaders as planters—men and women in whom you've invested significant time and resources—is an even more difficult decision and undertaking. To say this creates tension would be a gross understatement.

Multiplication is a disruptive force for the mother church, requiring ongoing recruiting and training of new staff. It results in far more disruption and turnover than the safety of addition. This energy-consuming reality can also affect staff quality and unity. The commitment to launch your best staff is a steep—and also Kingdom-building—price for mother church to pay.

This tension is at the heart of the emergence of a growing number of intern and residency programs for church planters. Multiplying churches realize that leadership development and a solid pipeline of leaders are essential.

Tension #9: Mother's Maturity vs. Baby's Birth

Should we wait until we're mature enough to plant a church, or begin moving forward now in planting?

Churches who want to plant other churches are wise to want to replicate spiritually mature and healthy cultures. If you have massive dysfunction in the mother church, then it may make sense to put any planting plans on hold. The question is, how mature must a church be before giving birth to a new church?

Naturally, leaders seek a sense of security before taking a risk in planting. They might assemble committees, commission studies or hire consultants to learn to plant most effectively. However, avoid "paralysis by analysis."

Walkemeyer points out: "Most churches are waiting too long to give birth. They fail to see that reproduction can be a means to maturity. There is nothing like becoming a parent to make you ready to be a parent. The most effective personal evangelists are not those who are fully trained and matured but rather, those who are newly saved. The same is true for multiplication. The younger and fresher a church is, the more apt it is to start another one. As churches age, they tend to become more averse to the adventures of multiplication."

Tension #10: Volunteer Talent Retention vs. Release

Should we hang on to our best volunteers, or send them out as church planters or part of a launch team?

In addition-growth culture, the demands of creating excellent programs to attract as many people as possible require retaining as many volunteer leaders as possible. Radically multiplying churches raise up leaders with a view toward releasing them into church plants versus retaining them long-term to build your bench. In rapidly multiplying churches, the "leaders' bench" might run less deep than they'd like because they're sending as many leaders out the door as quickly as they are equipped. Instead of stockpiling volunteer talent, these churches accept that there will be frequent "valley times" in the quantity and quality of leaders, particularly after sending out a significant-sized church plant.

Tension #11: Relational Stability vs. Relational Transience

Should we focus on developing the current social networks of friendship within the mother church or potentially disrupt those relationships through sending?

Planting a church can, and will, seriously disrupt existing social networks of friendship, especially when staff and volunteer leaders who demonstrate love and care for your church are sent out. Circles of friends can lose their cohesiveness as some friends go to seed the church plant, while others stay with the mother church. The temptation is to stop or slow planting so that the body can become more socially connected and attached to one another. If you're going to be a leader of a multiplying church, you must help your church understand the true basis for unity.

Tension #12: Systems Optimized vs. Systems Dispersed

Should we direct energy toward optimizing systems at the mother church, or toward the system and people at a new church plant?

Ministry excellence is a worthy goal. God deserves our very best, and as leaders we have to develop God-honoring systems through each ministry of our church. Multiplication culture-builders, though, are careful not to allow this pursuit of optimization to prevent them from releasing leaders and resources. When staff, leaders and workers are released for planting endeavors, systems are usually impacted in their operational efficiency. But take heart! This disruption allows your church to be disbursed to new places of growth.

Tension #13: Board Wisdom vs. Board Faith

Should our board lean more on cautious wisdom or risk-taking faith?

This tension depends on the polity and governance under which your church operates. Certainly, wisdom and faith are not opposites. They can, and should, coexist in the mind of a truly spiritual person. Though this tension is usually tied in some way to financial considerations, it is about much more than finances.

Church boards rightly concern themselves with church sustainability. When ministry actions that seemingly threaten sustainability are proposed, most boards have a natural protectiveness to resist. They cite the priority of wisdom: "God has given us brains to understand the realities we have to live with." Rare is the board that can reach forward in faith and risk what exists for the sake of Kingdom multiplication. These unique board leaders say, "This makes little sense in the natural, but we prayerfully believe God is going to back us up. Consequently, we will take action for Kingdom multiplication."

Tension #14: Proximity Protection vs. Proximity Evangelism
Should the mother church protect our "turf" by sending the plant far away, or trust that working together will create greater Kingdom impact?

You've probably heard the reasons for planting a certain distance (e.g., 30 minutes, 20 miles) away from the mother church:

- We don't want to saturate the market;
- You'll be competing with us;
- We need our best leaders to stay with us;
- "You don't want to be a 'sheep stealer,' do you?" etc.

Addition-growth culture might view the "fishing pool" as members of the mother church or existing Christian consumers looking for a new church in the local area. Leaders who respond from a multiplication worldview, though, believe the fishing pool consists of hungry unbelievers and the unchurched in the area. Rather than struggling with transfer growth, rapidly multiplying churches are planted for evangelism to the unreached—in which case, even more churches could be planted in that area.

Tension #15: Highly Educated Planters vs. Spiritually Empowered Planters

Should our planters rely on accumulated knowledge or activated faith?

Because church planting is such a demanding undertaking, you'll naturally want to equip planters as much as possible. Inevitably, multiplying churches will face this tension: "Who is ready to plant? We should not send out a planter until they are fully equipped, seminary trained, theologically and intellectually astute, fully prepared for the work." However, be careful not to reinforce a false dichotomy between lay leaders and the "paid professionals." Don't hobble multiplication at the gate by creating non-scriptural qualifications for who can and cannot plant.

The other extreme bases qualifications on those who are saved, gifted, able to gather people, enthusiastic and evangelistic—and therefore, ready to be sent. In the urgency of sending planters, though, be sure not to hinder planting by sending out zealous yet unqualified leaders who undermine healthy multiplication in the long term.

Tension #16: Filling Existing Churches vs. Starting New Churches

Should we prioritize revitalizing existing churches, or begin planting new churches?

For most planters, the reality is that there will already be local churches in the area where they feel called to plant. And many of those existing churches will be in need of revitalization. Multiplying leaders are open to collaborating with and blessing other local churches, but are not constrained by the needs of those existing churches. We should aggressively look for the opportunities to collaborate in planting and revitalization, rather than pitting the two against each other.

Tension #17: Missional Focus vs. Multiplication Focus
Should we address the needs of our neighborhood before starting a church, or address the community's needs at the same time as planting?

Walkemeyer writes about this tension and shares what he has learned through Light & Life Fellowship's multiplication journey: "The missional nature of the Church is undeniable. We are saved to serve, to demonstrate the tangible Kingdom, to be salt and light where God has placed us. However, when that becomes an argument against the multiplication of churches, we have overthrown our point. Do we care for the poor *or* evangelize the lost? The answer is *yes*. As soon as the missional and multiplication become competitive, we have misunderstood the nature of both."

Multiplying leaders recognize God's heart for the poor and see that a missional emphasis can be the impetus for starting new churches. Out of missional expressions of the existing church, new churches can rise up and multiply missional endeavors.

Tension #18: Missions Focus vs. Multiplication Focus
Should we direct resources to global missions or to local church planting?

In response to the call to radical multiplication, you'll likely experience others' hesitation. It might go something like this: "Why should we start new churches to tell people about Jesus when there are numerous ways for Americans to hear the gospel? Most have heard it multiple times. Instead, we need to focus on taking the gospel to those who have never heard it for the first time!"

Multiplying leaders refuse to believe that resources dedicated to local church planting will detract from global missions. These leaders believe every new church has the potential to become a resource for global missions.